More Advance Praise for Raven King

"Incandescent, scathing. A lyrical anti-fairytale. A conjuring. To open this book is to wander the rural churchyards and railyards of upstate NY; to speak with Erzsébet Báthory, the centuries-dead Hungarian female serial killer; to meet spirit mediums, seers, grieving mothers, witches of all kinds. *Raven King* is an indictment of the spiritual sickness that causes gendered violence, an elegy for all of the girls and women we have lost to the disease, and a lovesong for the female friendships that sustain us through times of darkness."

—Mary McMyne, author of *The Book of Gothel* and *Wolf Skin*

"With sumptuous titles that remind us how complex the contexts of our emotions sometimes seem, how at odds and in tune with the immediacy of the body; and with refrains that evoke a melody of wanderlust, the poems in *Raven King* declare for us that the resilience of the goddess burns in every woman. These poems glide through the liminal spaces of the spirit, weaving grief and rage, wielding vulnerability like a righteous blade afire with ravenous conviction. The heritage of past twines with the stark candor of the present, a feather-hued skull, a vine rendered from dream, recalling to us that violence has always been the rope walked by women at the hands of men, and that it does not need to be the tether keeping them from the fulfillment of a desire to embrace the freedom of wilderness and empowerment. In this collection, listen to the Medusa's laugh, and love the haunting ricochet of its turn to stony song in these lyrical, lithe, and luminous words."

—Dr. Saba Syed Razvi, author of *heliophobia* and *In the Crocodile Gardens*

RAVEN KING

RAVEN KING

POEMS

BY

FOX HENRY FRAZIER

Yes Poetry Books
Brooklyn, NY

Published by Yes Poetry Books
Brooklyn, NY
http://yespoetry.com

Cover art by Jen Stein Hauptman (Instagram: @jensteinpoet).
Mixed media, digital painting, 2021. Image used by kind permission of the artist.

All interior illustrations by Joanna C. Valente. Mixed media, 2021.
Image used by kind permission of the artist.

All photographs in "I Live in the Shadow Hills" taken by Fox Henry Frazier.
Used by kind permission.

Author photograph by Jessie Coleman Photography (Instagram: @GoForJessie), 2021.
Image used by kind permission of the photographer.

Book Designer: Sarah Reck
Editor: Joanna C. Valente

This title is available for purchase directly from the publisher.

Library of Congress
Cataloguing-in-Publication Data

Raven King // Fox Henry Frazier
Library of Congress Control Number 2021948014
Frazier, Fox Henry
ISBN 978-0-578-99540-3

9 8 7 6 5 4 3 2 1
FIRST EDITION

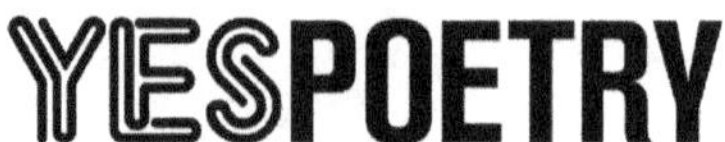

"Girls can wear jeans and cut their hair short and wear shirts and boots because it's okay to be a boy; for girls, it's like a promotion. But for a boy to look like a girl is degrading, according to you, because secretly you believe that being a girl is degrading."

—Ian McEwan, *The Cement Garden*

"My servant tells me you have occupied my estate in Lindva. I do not understand. Why have you done this thing? Do not think that I am just another Widow; believe me, I will not keep silent. I will let no one take my property. I just wanted you to know this: Do not think I shall leave you to enjoy it. You will find a man in me."

—Erzsébet Báthory, in a 1606 letter to a Count who had usurped her property to intimidate her

Contents

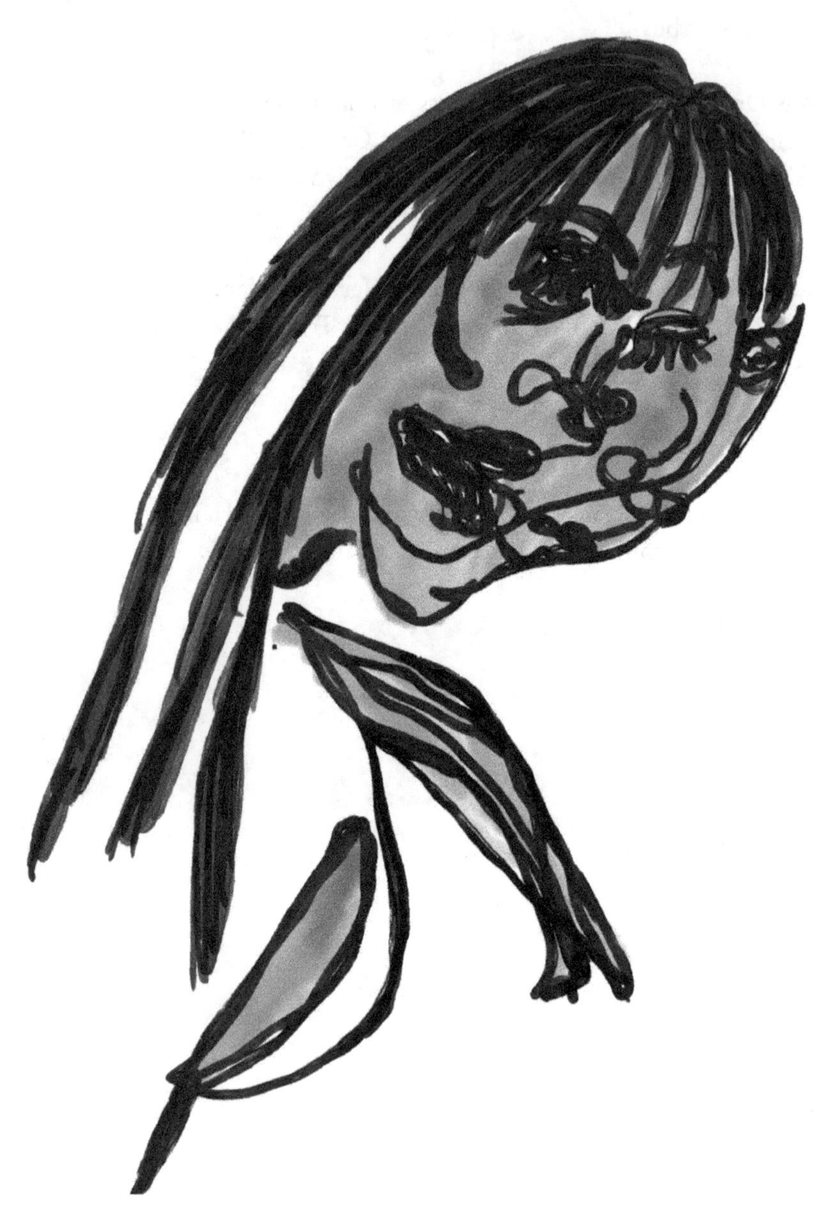

Exodus in X Minor

He pulled me from the sea: lush siren, laced
in waves. Cradled me in his arms, carried me through
Luna Park—red bulbs lighting abandoned steel

tower like a spasm, ghosts of those who'd
jumped spiraling past. A mother, sea-

haired & wheeling her twins. Flying its
Jolly Iago flag high, one wooden ship
making clumsy turns in the bay.   *I love you,*

he repeated for months, incantation to summon
me into that most desired form of desire.

I bought a phonograph that summer. He said we
had no space for it. That it was *trying too hard.*
I wandered alone by the sea, through tattoo parlors,

boardwalk clusters of amphibian scales & feathered creatures,
towards the man with a beard around his eyelids, too shy

to flirt with him because he had groupies. Raccoons gnawed
at dumpster detritus with gleeful abandon. *When they show*
you their teeth, they're not smiling. There was a double-headed

deer trophy, a woman who could ignite gasoline
with her tongue, whose companion python

contentedly slid its charmed head between her
teeth. The sleek silver sword self-inserted—down her
throat, between her lungs, into her belly, the soft

gust as I pulled it out when she pointed at me and winked.
I think you love that place more than you love me, he said.

He knelt before me there, one night, fell over as our Wonder
Wheel car glided out—shooting us like stars into the Brooklyn
dark, the rock back a surprise every time. Suddenly, I was back

in Assateague under a bright willow, sky growing lavender
with rain and dusk. *I'd go anywhere,* he said,

and the ring sparkled   just so.   I slid my
arms around his impatient, wobbling girth, pulled
him West.   Inside the secret cavern of my body, I kept

setting that phonograph needle to vinyl,
hot summer jazz reverberating through me alone as I stared at the sea,

until the record died, and the player
remained, arm reaching towards its own silent
core as if by memory. By heart, as by mistake.

The Raven-Haired Seer Visits St. Francis Farm, Run by Catholic Workers in Upstate NY, with the Great-Granddaughter of the Farm's Original Founders

You're so delicate, Magdalena laughed, rubbed her nose
white with plaster dust, oblivious, snatched the hammer

from my hand. *This isn't a tea party, babe. Go see*
to the kids. The children gathered at my side, unbidden,

Mags tossing her hair and power drill around next to the dry
walls we'd freshly constructed to save the mother downstairs from

a fresh custody battle with her alcoholic ex. I imagined touching
Magdalena's cheek with my French manicured fingertips, slowly taking

the drill from her hand, then slamming the bit into the wall
beside her head, catching a bit of her hair in the whir. Instead, I took

Ashley and Brian blackberry picking in their backyard. I made them
bubble wands from wire coat hangers, and they more or less threw

soap at each other while I washed every dish in the place. Brett, their older
(and really their half-)brother, listened to white-supremacist punk-rock at his

stereo's top volume the entire time and wouldn't talk to anyone. I didn't mind
being ignored, but the music really pissed me off. It also made me think he might

molest his little sister, although that was probably reactionary & unfounded.
Ashley and Brian showed me the room in which they shared a bed

because there was no room for a second. There was some kind of cross-
stitched thing on the wall, which Ashley said their grandmother had made.

It had a rhyme about children being special to Jesus. Below it
was a toybox with exactly three toys in it: one skeletal artifact

of a GI Joe, one threadbare puppy with a mildewed ear who was losing
his insides, and one—I think it was—doll, which appeared

to be plastic, most of its painted features rubbed off. In some places
it was translucent. When it was time to leave, I got into the commune

truck and knew we were on our way to smoke up in the Chapel like we
did most evenings. *Come read Simone with me,* I'd say, holding my

hand out to Mags as she stood over me, wrapped in a towel, rolling
a joint with her free hand as she tickled my fingers with the other. *You make*

too many rules for yourself, babe, she'd say, and I'd appreciate how clean
her hair looked, how undamaged, when it was too damp to force

into feral contortions and instead hung in relaxed
waves. Her eyes green and startlingly crooked, bangs

curling awkwardly, smile jagged though she'd finally
stopped biting her lips. *The Second Sex* would drop

from my grip onto the shag carpet next to me for a moment
as I received the lit joint from her, fresh as a kiss, but I'd always

pick it up again, shrugging, *Suit yourself,* while Mags took the J and lay
next to me, finally quiet, and I could pretend we were both at peace. I finished

reading my book the following week, in Paris. I saw the Eiffel tower
every night from my balcony; the light display, new at that point,

seemed tacky even to me. The curtains blew into the room and back
perfectly, the one night we had a thunderstorm—the same night I first

dreamed of building a home with Mags. In my dream, she
vanishes and I search, finding only that sad toy box. I raise my

eyes to the wall hanging, and somehow manage to pull the power
drill from under the bed. I grab Mags by her hair and yank her

back to me, exasperated. *Stop fucking around and do*
what you're supposed to, for once, I snap. Her hair

transmogrifies to cross-stitch in my hand just as I push
the whirling drill-bit through, back and forth until I'm holding

a pile of thin, crimped yarn. Ashley comes up behind me
and says, *Where's Jesus?* (meaning, of course, the mangled

needlepoint, but she says *Jesus*) and I say, *Exactly,* fearing that Ashley
might take the drill from me and shove it through my spinning brain,

or maybe pierce her palms. I disappear the drill and say into her face,
I tried, my words moving as though underwater.   In another ten

years, and not in a dream, Mags will call me
          from rehab, asking for money so she can rebuild

her heroin habit safely, once she gets out and gets
          her kids back. *I only need*

a little, she'll say, and I will
          hang up the phone.   *I tried,*

I tell Ashley again, tossing half-awake in my Parisian sheets, lightning
crashing outside on the terrace. I plunge back under: *I think this*

belongs to you, she says, handing me my deBeauvoir book. *No*,
I say, *you keep it*, holding it back out to her as a gift, but she's already

gone, swimming across the house we helped build her
like a dance. I pause in the doorway; she giggles, sing-

songing after me, *This isn't a tea party. You make the rules*
here, babe. Stop being so delicate. Learn to look after the kids.

Letter to Diane Arbus

Some among us are always thumbing absently for the worn

horn of a saddle in our memory, teeth

clenched against the cold of that snowful skyline blown so sleek you can't

discern river from road.

(Or: dying

to make love in a wax body

museum.)

and the coroner find in my

cardiac muscle that kernel of

(singer-sewing contest, soap box derby, eating or drinking (pie watermelon), diaper derby palisades, walkathon St Louis, chess champ, miss appetite, miss fluidless contact lens, yeast raised donut queen, miss peel appeal natl idaho potato week, tooth health week queen, miss press photog, miss antifreeze, miss saltwater taffy wk)

As a child, I dressed

one October as a crash

test dummy.

The Raven-Haired Cartographers' Daughter First Encounters the Sunny-Haired Undertaker's Daughter When They Are Both Small Children

From wild October sunflower fields to slate-
grey asphalt plain, Matilda and Mélusine crossed

paths as stones made to ricochet by some all-
knowing hand. A legion of children flanked

Matilda, dawn-colored hair like a small war
banner billowing behind her body. Veering

from course to find Mélusine among the pines,
small palms extended. *Will you join*? Divergent

opinions flung between them about the evergreen
grove. Whose? How could we decide? We shared

a childish quest—to witness eidolon,
encounter our own sublime dry

ice ephemera distilled from thick & heavy
shapes we drag around with us. These bodies.

Wind whirling every needled sprig
like a surge, a ripple of small children

began to cry in chorus as we described the soul.
I'm the only one here who's seen a ghost,

Matilda said, and Mélusine's secrets
unspooled, grew thin and fluid in the cold

October air. *Look—this lady wrapped all*
shiny-soft and white, like pillow scars.

Someone dropped her in cold fog
& green needles and forgot

Mélusine's hand extended; Matilda cautiously

touched the redwood face, fantastic chenille-
knotted limbs. Pink and white silk chiffon sleeves

beat in the wind, glacial shiver of agitated
wings: *We're the only two,* Matilda said. We were.

As the Raven-Haired Seer Enters Her Teenage Years, Two Slightly Older Girls In A Nearby Town Are Tortured and Killed by Their Neighbor, Who Allegedly Commits Suicide in Jail Immediately After His Arrest

fancied ourselves astronauts
spelunkers in our
hearts dying to throw
what flares down that abyss

He took two girls and fastened
their limbs, folded them into
his trunk like poached fauna.

our parents used words like *evil*
sin meant *there are no*
reasons meant h*e baited us*
without a hook

ensconced ourselves in salted
circle splashed with more
holy water first growl candles'

stutter fingers gripping each
other's flesh: don't
break the circle—

He drove them through forest.
Made a fire. Slow, long heat.
Slow, long bleeds. God's silence.

took newspapers from us said, *there is no reason*
for you to know
meant *we are in a state*
of emergency *and fear* *we will remain*

second growl came clawing
a twisted, wintering hand we drawered
our candles fast dreamed them sycamore
sapling, lark where they'd been sown

He hurt them. He cut them
to pieces as their pulses beat

God's silence

they said he hanged himself in jail
knelt his weight against a shoelace
stretched to noose, meaning

no reason to ask *when justice has come*
calling at last *no*
reason you should ever know what it means

God's silence *to be that kind*
of alone

As the Raven-Haired Seers Enters Adulthood, She Changes Her Hair Color to Match Her Namesake, Hoping to Augment Her Vulpine Aptitude for Blending and Eluding in the Name of Survival

My body harvested darkness
in quantities it could not contain, crowned

itself with glossy black curls, opened

its portals to commune with the unborn

The cardinal I knew from two winters past
nested on my family's land   landed near my resting hand kept

my gaze rapt   *I'm with you   when you   see this*
said one of my blood   departed, and I wept.   I took, that spring,

to sleeping   in the four-poster bed
Aunt Margaret had left me when she died, woke

in the night to her   confusion   *why*
have you come to find me here in the dark, child   I received

letters   from a soldier
who'd   survived

serving in Iraq: *I dreamed   that you*
gave
me your teeth   to protect me

but who was I
to protect?

My neighbors, Valerie and Devin, were murdered
inside their suburban home. Devin, 14, had gone to
Maryland to help her sister Tammie, and Tammie's
husband, Vernon, with their new baby. On the drive
back to upstate New York, Devin told her sister about
the way Vernon had cornered her, taken her
into the basement, touched her, removed her
clothing. Vernon, a truck driver and recently
self-styled bounty hunter, reacted to the police
charges by calling his friend, Robert. Robert was
also an autodidactic bounty hunter. They got their
guns, and drove north together, to this sleepy
vampiric little town with its beautiful pastoral
rivers and hills. Vernon and Robert broke
into Valerie's stately home, brick with red and
cream gingerbread trim, and a second-floor balcony
which they pulled Devin from. She tried to defend
herself and her mother with a baseball bat, so these
two men threw this little girl down a flight of stairs,
barking, "This is personal," forced mother and
daughter both into the basement, where they
made them lie facedown, then shot them nine
times in their backs and in the back of their heads.

I drove myself
past the yellow-black taped brick
daily. How many times could I
think about holding my breath?

A fox stopped running down the road one day, and turned to eye me fully.

How many more fitful nights of late
aunts murmuring, puzzling, questioning, pushing me waking
red-

eyed   red veins spread like cracks, lids
puffing shut   could I sustain? How to levee this

dark tide, hide   from what I saw
what I held inside   so I

incarnadined my mane, reincarnated
myself to match   my name   maybe

now I could relax

into what

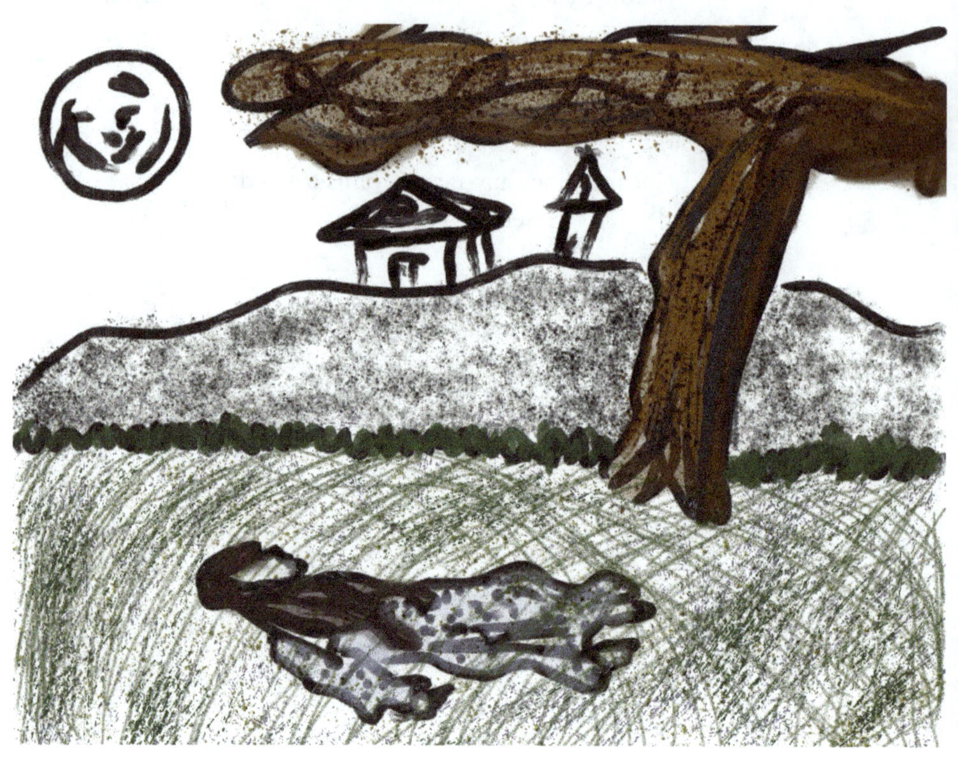

The Fox-Haired Seer Visits a Natural-Born Spirit Medium in Troy, NY, and They Visit the Grave of Hazel Drew, Who Was Bludgeoned and Drowned in Teal's Pond in 1908

Stone mortared on stone till it turns into hillside
          fortress holding clash of rose gold

          haired sylph who spits poems, possessed
her electric   her fresh   her blue walled   spirit—Water

boiled and poured: resurrecting hibiscus,
          raising its scent and its pink

          to mouths languid and anxious, hard-
carved and stirring, to speak the unspeakable

visions without a within. Wood that springs
          open, releases floor into ceiling: trap

          door's staircase unfolding a hundred
years past: clothespins still metal-cinched, smooth

& heavy in circumspect palms. (I did ask
          permission. And could) hear the question not asked,

          the stone never placed on her finger, its glint
on the pale wifely hand that scratched its own palm

imbrued, crying those lucid nights trying
          to scry wherever he went. Water boiled and poured out to melt

impurities from discarded garments, rent
as the night by a cry or a moan

in those rooms rented out by night
down the hall; darkest

corridor of trees on the long
walk past Teal's Pond, hunters

gathered among them, silent, seeking the common
joy of taking whatever stealthy sleek bodies

they found and then found they could
keep. Water that parts to make way, then

churning back, mixes
flesh with its depth, and falls still.

Woods veiling the violence through thicket and quick
unidentified creature darting through brush. Found stone:

glittering as a sweet-drawled
hello, beautiful,   embedded

in skull like a wake. White granite, carved
to read *Hazel,* vined flowers, her dates. Water

sprinkled from sky as if scattered from palm
leaves, baptismal, upon us. The thick, lightning-

scarred trunk of an oak, sacred portal; its lichen
in patches, the lives of her parents, their grief

still husking the air. Wood chopped and dismembered
          to timber, screwed into new shapes to hold sacred

          quotidian book of litanies for the itinerant. My own marble
stones quarried verdant in Clifden, tumbled

& burnished to prayer beads & strung
          like sobs, through my fingers, a voice

          still pleading for Mother as water
streams scalding before mixing in the bathtub

with cold, the waves made
          by a body easing in.

Exodus in X Minor

Dear Iago:

I will not be foreshadowed by the serpentine
beauty whose mouth you slit to fit fire-

crackers in, boy with tingling fingers breaking body to
trophy, detonated jade pieces, dust-nestling.

I like to sleep in trains & in beds
not my own, and as you'd expect, I make

no apology for that. I've been lying to you about missing
sugar: I crave unsweetened cocoa-bitter coffee after hours

lost in a hailstorm among the Gothic
architectures of an unfamiliar city (Prague, if

you want to know). Born as if swaddled
red in the tethers of existence itself, some us learned

as children that cold for the first
time passes straight, plate-like, through the body

and we couldn't get enough of it.
As though this enclosure in the world makes us

slam against each other like igneous
particles inside a volcano, frenetically heating, kinetic

our natural state. *Fernweh,* the Germans say, distance pain,
a homesickness for the horizon. That, yes,

but beyond it: I wake to cigarettes streaking the air
like rancid incense in Sorrento (and you know

I have asthma), the rasp & choke a halo of gold-edged
purple-drenched orchids, when my memory measures

it against your vomit pillow, your somnolent
urine capillarying its way to my

skin through shared sheets. Please forget
that I ever curled into you like a cat seeking

shelter from rain. I *love* rain. The way you love
bourbon. The way you will stumble until you run

out of earth. Keep your pink make-up
peonies, geometries of memory in glass

bubbles adorning table & sill.
I belong to futures, now. And will.

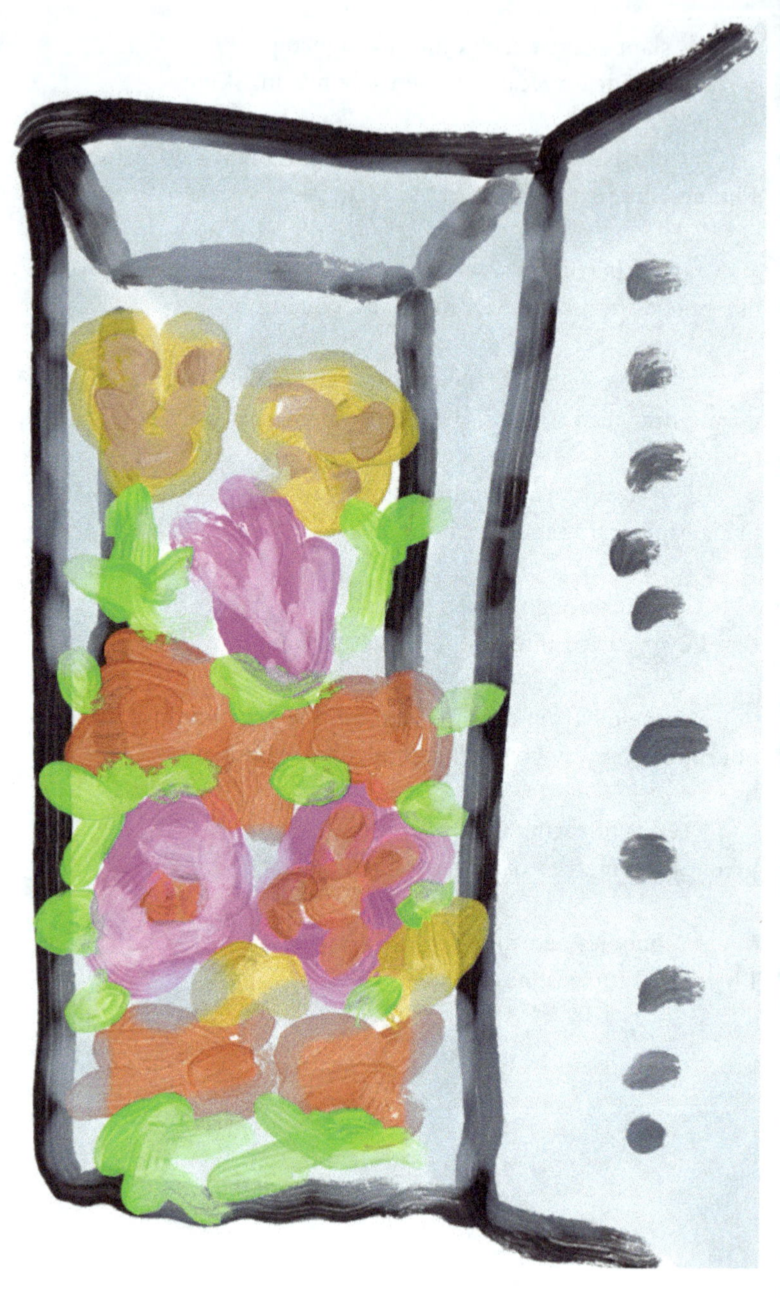

For Maddy Lerner, Age 6, Accidentally Killed at an Outdoor Firing Range in Upstate New York

Dear Madison, I was told of your death
over dinner. You were, they said, struck

by hot brass from your mother's new
AR-15 with custom scope. A tiny girl

at the table behind ours hit
the lights and the television

glowed in the dim like
when Miss Brassi turned

off the movie of Medea, and there
was a wispy, blue-lidded anchor

saying Columbine, school pictures
across the screen. Bryan Andrews

was handing me a piece
of gum. He paused, snorted,

said, They look like dorks.
Maddy, when I was your age,

Andy Boyle brought bullets
to show & tell. He got detention

and a beating. The waitress
brought our bangers & mash.

My first trip to London, Clive
told us that four weeks after

the preschool episode
in Scotland, all of the

handheld kind were
banned. One woman

from New Jersey volunteered, *That*
would never work where I'm from,

and Clive said, *Of course not,*
you all think you're cowboys.

That fall, my friends and I left
daisy wreaths on the armory steps.

When he heard, my ROTC
boyfriend said, *It's the year 2000*

and there won't be
any more wars. If this

is what you think of me,
forget it. Gas is expensive,

and left me in the rainy lot.
The next morning he filled

my locker with flowers.
Maddy, I'm scared

to ask how they feel
in the meat of you: the shells

fell warm against
my hand & I saved

the target to hang in my fire
escape window that won't lock.

When they asked over dessert
how the first shot felt, I thought

of you & said, *I'd never held
a gun before today*. The souvenir

shell in my purse, I said,
It was great, which felt like

saying, *I'm tough*. Like saying,
I have nothing to do with this.

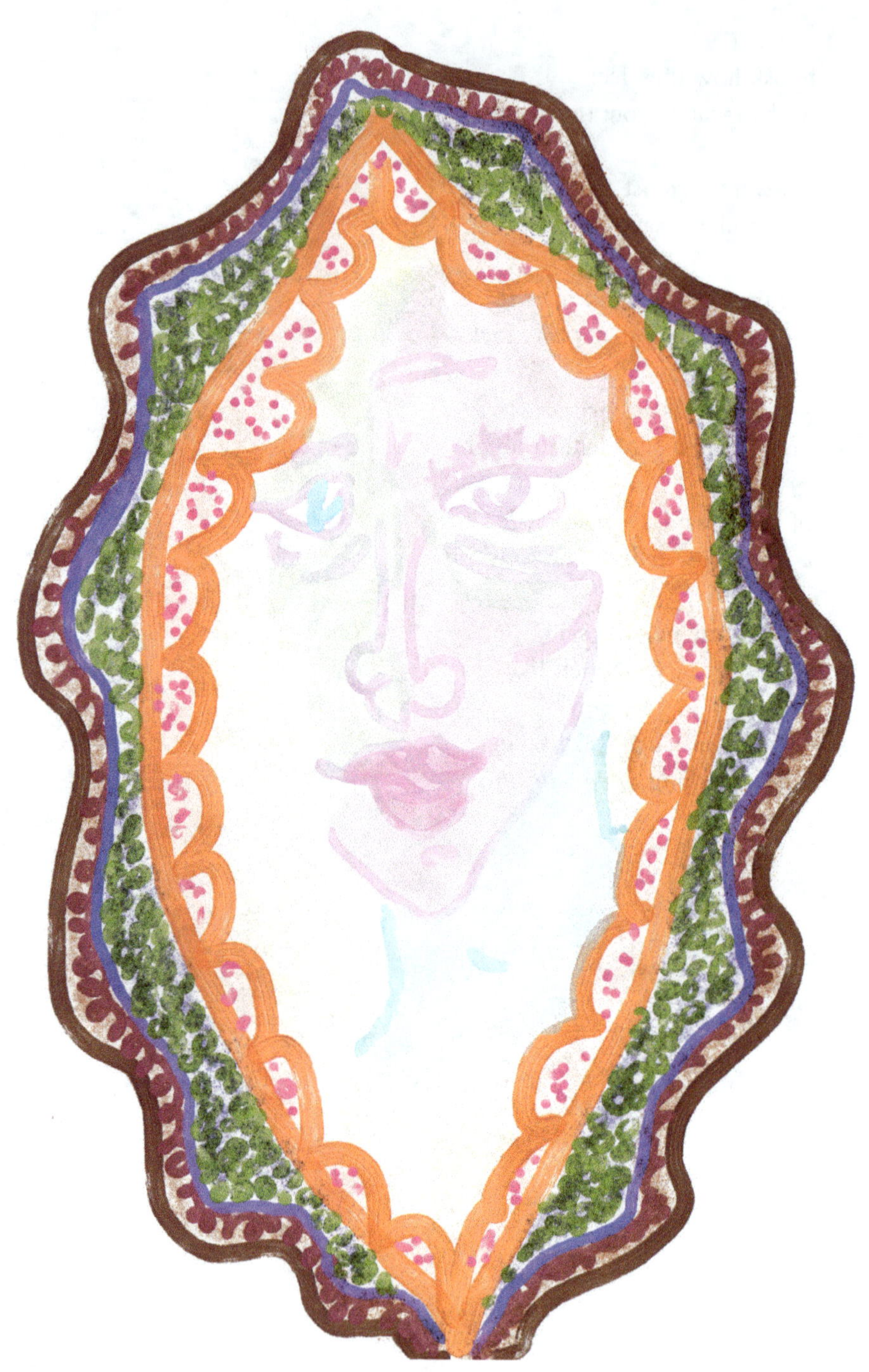

Letter to Diane Arbus

you consumed

like a twin

in the womb (Museum

it in a bottle: axolotl

in formaldehyde, sterile

& staring, perilous as a novice
bride of Christ).

The Raven-Haired Seer Dreams of a Girl Her Age, Abducted from a Nearby Road, and Keeps the Dreams to Herself Until She Begins to Dream Too of the Abducted Girl's Murderer

If forty-seven locusts in my mouth I could
not talk   her hair in wind   like mine

If water tastes of blood we need more
water   she laughed   she never

looked right at me

If we are the water and the locusts
let us pray   how   could this   how   could I

how

If we are wretched wrested deep
in prayer   let us   I dreamed

his glasses   mustache   dreamed

they found him   dreamed   forty days

of darkness would begin if I said his name out loud   They did find him, my father said, last night while

you slept If boils burn our eyelids covered

his mouth, kept If rivers rise & loose our city

walls If God cannot bring Himself to keep

his eyes on the grey our children safe from this

being taken this

grey expanse before us

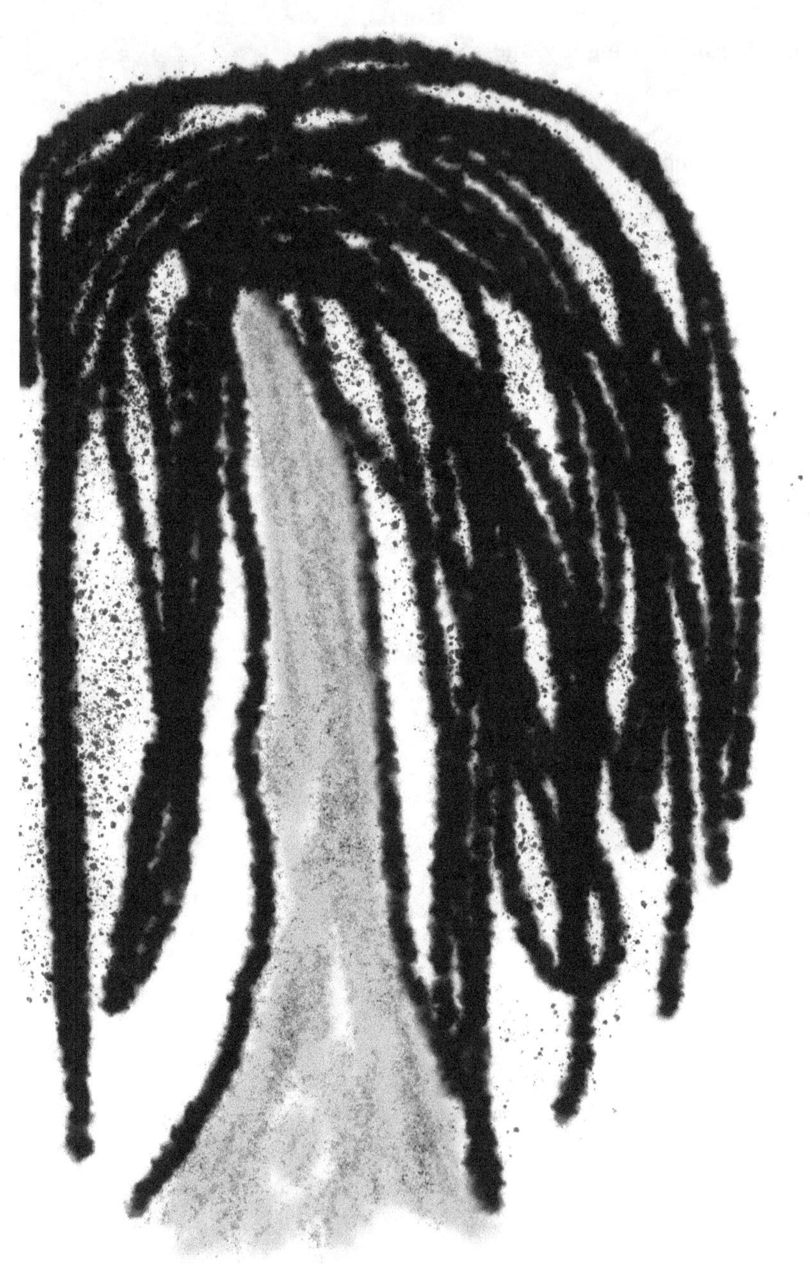

The Fox-Haired Seer Makes A Pilgrimage to Devil's Elbow, NY, Where in 1932 A Steam-Shovel Operator Discovered the Skull of an Axe-Murdered Young Woman; and Listens

Not unlike the Vestals in their forced
walks across Rome to prove their bodies

unviolated by men, I conduct my
promenade: body both water and sieve,

both returned to the earth and ignited
by rage.   Delicate, I   lift my skirt

safeguarding lacy train from smeared
detritus   catching.   Extend my gentle hand

to metallic, phallic chariots whizzing
past; beckon them pause & deliver me

(hot tongue spreading to all-
consuming inferno)   that infamous, grooved

valved muscle still spilling bright
waters, chameleon-like, the blue

flooding purple then scarlet, cherry-dark,
ripe-apple sweet.   I'll suck them like they've

never dreamed, until they lose
the road, their poor

skulls spiderwebbing
on force of impact. I thumb

each eye closed with a smile as each
man rests like an unborn calf

against the steering wheel:
milky, still.   I won't

lie: there are the precious,
few who stop in rain and open the door meaning me

no harm at all. Their gentle hearts flicker through
my gasping core—burn like distilled spirit—violent

as white powder lit.   I can't take them. I let them
blink to find my voice was merely some unearthly

tone of wind, visage a mistake in the brain—
Woman but a pattern forged by blizzard blur

or their own rich somnambulant vision. False
witness borne against themselves, they scurry

home to dark abodes & light too many rooms, wrap
too-cold corpora in quilts   never smothering that new

quake in the limbs. They dream
of a paper doll transforming

into smoke, burnt by a brutal boy
after he's finished making her

scraps with his blade.
My last moments illuminate

before me like Leda's
smothered convulsions

against downy breast, the cleaved
immortality that comes

After.   *And so I take you, beloved,* the men used
to say to those young girls they'd chosen

to serve Vesta. Then swathed them in gauzy
atrophy, not unlike my own laced-up ennui

though, unlike them, I can change
my clothes, at least—sequins & tulle, late

for what the girls now call prom, lost
& helpless chiffon-draped debutante, sad

abandoned bride drowning in taffeta sobs, my
own true   boned & stayed silk   corseted snowy

shape—postured, controlled, abject in all
but my appetites.   I consecrate

myself & stare   deep   well of grief
fracked flammable   I conflagrate

gift to my daughters who walk
home alone at night   gibbous

reds and yellows eradicating
each other   within   let tongues

consume the lamb
            flickering   ravenous   silent

save the sporadic, inveterate
            ferocious   susurrate   *I am*

Exodus in X Minor

whiskey-shooting copperhead prodigal

newly stripped needling
bodied surreptitious ink one delicious

brunette bartender mixes all my martinis & Xanax

lets me sleep at last another, gravel-throated & strawberry
blonde, picks bluegrass after hours *Won't you*

bury me beneath the tree where my family lies my family's

scattered below the Mason-Dixon line parents errant
self-made orphans who wandered into this overcast vortex

& shipped me yearly home to grandmother's Bittersweet Farm erstwhile, late

doctor's estate haunted, the seller insisted by a red-bearded plantation
owner who had enslaved women broke their bodies, made them

widows took their babies until their grief summoned spirits

to boil his brain inside his skull my grandmother said I'*m not*
afraid of evil men. He'll have to leave or hide from me and signed *Won't you*

bury me I sleep on the brunette's mattressed floor to hide

from the red-bearded man who hurts me   says *only when you*
tell me to   meaning *I can do whatever I want to (break) you*

ensconced in her

damp comforter: dreams of the night I was six
or seven, and saw him—I saw him

wandering the halls of the big house with a candle   harmless

in his white   starched nightshirt   I didn't know
enough to fear him

There are no

such things as ghosts is something mother
never told me   *beneath the tree where my family*

lies   father's best friend was stabbed to death

in front of him last year, one year after a gun-
man stormed the community center of this cloudy town

and murdered 13 people   one year after this red-

bearded man   the one who would   find me   and hold fast
sat across the street, shooting

whiskey   laughing with friends   now he runs

his hand over his chin   at daybreak   reading the text
on his phone   another stripper he used to sell coke to

is dead from heroin   *I think of it as suicide,* he says

he didn't cry when Kevin's
skull was split in the street by a truck at 3 a.m.

that red-leafed month he left us *won't you bury me*

I drive to Friendsville, past Quaker Lake, three times
a week with my dog: rural churchyards, fallen

leaves streams occasional blown hay straw mist I always

return before dark in truth I fear even those who tremble with love
or fear of God *beneath the tree* the red-bearded ghost

never hurt me I circled myself with salt & wished he would

prove himself real had nightmares in which he did
woke up terrified satisfied My father watched his friend

carried out of his office a corpse, the guilty

student in handcuffs knife on the floor *where*
my family lies My father said, Go to

sleep, I won't let anything hurt you Oh my red-

bearded man holds me
tightly by my throat & I

relax My red-bearded man cuts me

another line it is dark
by 4 p.m. in this town *Hear the willow's cries.*

Erzsébet Báthory Visits the Fox-Haired Seer in a Dream and Reveals How She Learned Her Aristocratic Family's Concepts of Justice as a Young Girl, When a Peasant Who Sold His Daughter into Slavery was Executed Before Her

I never saw her, nor her noble
buyer but for her

purchase like a loaf
or goat
we sewed

him into warm
slit belly
of horse.

It brayed weakening kicked
I saw her then laced with a bit

he squirmed inside, it lay
chuffing for death

he spun within I saw her
twisting in rope enveloped by hot

what does a man want with buying a girl

riding home   I stared, bared my too-
wide eyes through the windows of the coach

an unkindness   consuming carrion   far from road

I remembered my father handing me a flower: blue tulle

petals like a paternal kiss
like the calm   absence of need

like the power to say, *Hush. All shall be well.*

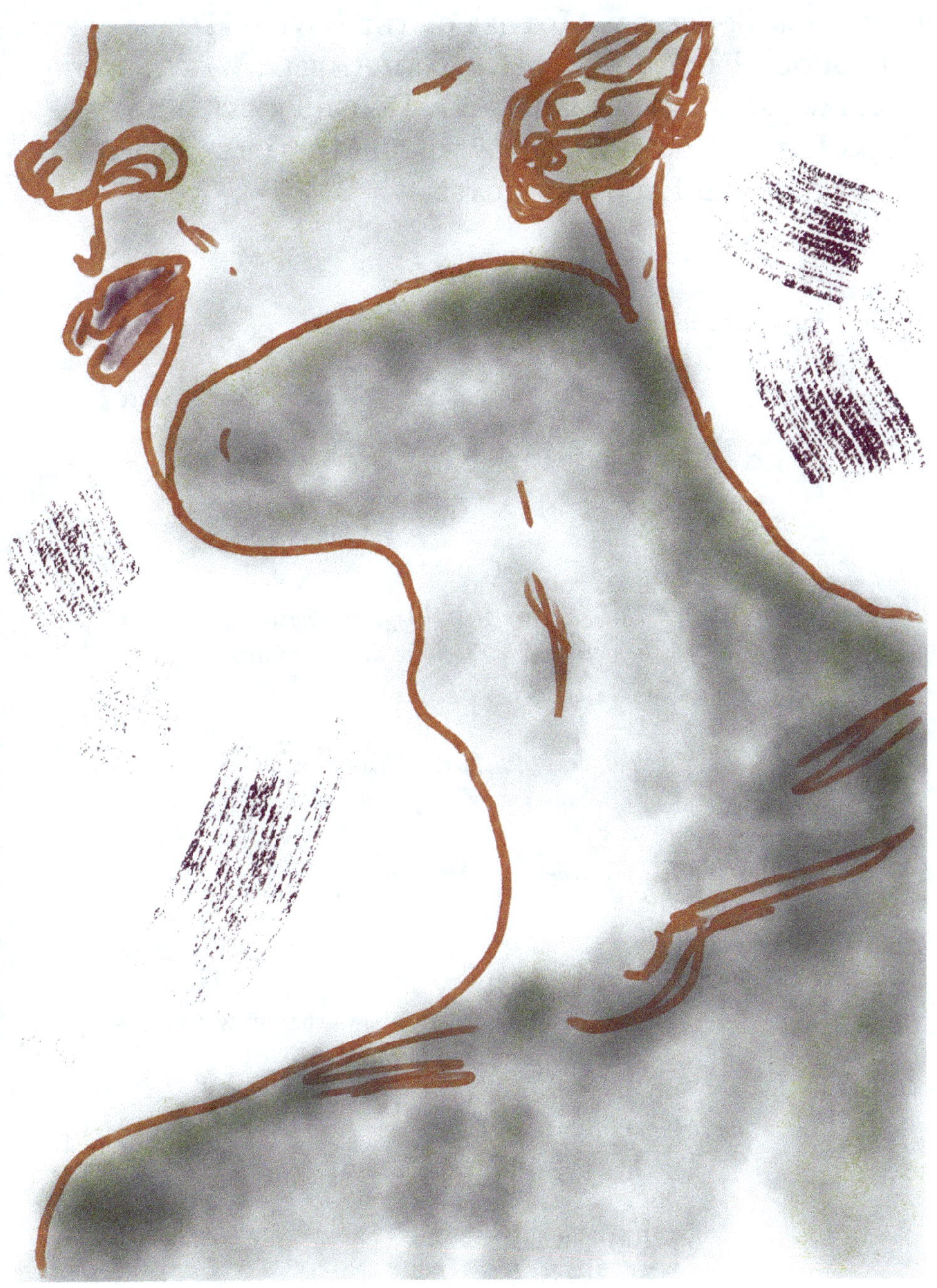

Gretchen Foggerty, Mother of the Raven-Haired Seer's Childhood Friends Philomena and Amelia, Was Arrested for Harassing Father Roderick, Parish Priest Who Years Later Would Be Arrested on Multiple Charges of Pedophilia and Excommunicated

she thrashed she undressed

his rectory room, shirt

by shirt shoe by shoe

This belt, my girls, keeps me chaste.
Sometimes I do feel the urge. I admit

your beautiful faces. *Examine*
your consciences' *truth*: *what*

have you wanted—

she flailed, she assaulted

homily service pews she threw
her body facedown in the aisle

he strips them in school,
she sang, dancing backwards.

Face tilted:
My child.

Who regarded us? Rapt
captives of pulpit.

Opiated. Apt. Exalted

He said suffer them unto me   he said I tell you: sow a thought,

reap an action

by fountain & silence   whose festering kindness

Who bled & who learned

of alchemy's black: the sore, the burn,

that Wound plunging deep in the side

rendered whole as stained glass: bright slivers

of feather, of water, of fern
(the bullet implied)

sow an action, reap a habit

whose core cracked

sow a habit, reap a destiny

& brittle as the breast
bone of a bittern

Daniel Was One of Four Catholic Workers in Ithaca, New York, Who Spilled His Blood at a Military Recruitment Center in Protest of the USA's Invasion of Iraq, and Was Subsequently Arrested and Imprisoned

Cachexia collects its echoes:
my sacred cache of chambers.

Breath is hymn. Is He. Vermilion
   cataclysm   walled calligraphy:

refuse   silence   flood   currency
of speech   These divided reach

for relics weighed & measured,
wanting the crude,   the stark

the fractured Temple. Insatiable
   scions of sciamachy, I am still

but breathe among these
stirring lions in the dark.

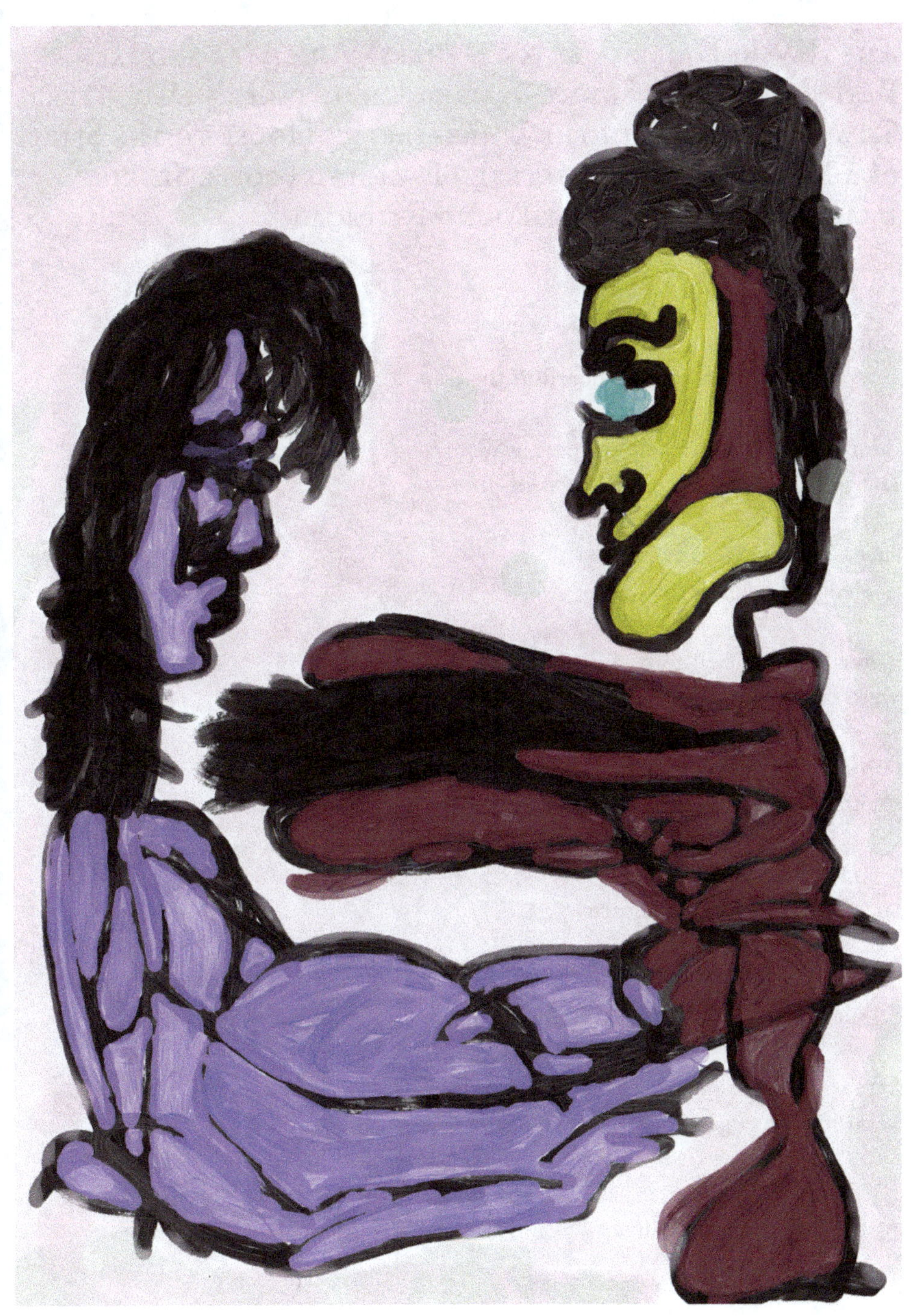

The Raven-Haired Cartographers' Daughter and Her Best Friend, the Sunny-Haired Undertaker's Daughter, Speak One Night in the Undertaker's House to the Spirit of a Minister Who Sheltered Enslaved People Seeking Freedom on the Underground Railroad

Our seventh winter, we smuggled
        candles, a lettered board to the trap-

doored stairs behind her bedroom wall.
Did you get caught? Did the families find

each other at Niagara Falls?
    All the colors of white

water flinging itself to rock
were in our silence. We were

surprised by his kindness, his
Your secret doorway is a gift

    Could we lose, and if
so, what?   Our hearts

pounded into sleep. Rosy
   silent   porcelain girls collected

shreds   of whisper   shards of witnessed
  hush   and   gasp   on fastened shelves

        unblinking   in luminous
painted skin   in chintz

and lace   folds of dusty
dresses   silent

save the gathered
echoes   of soaked-lung screams

We woke   halfway to each
other's murmurs,   drifted

among reddened leaves   hounds
stopped by ice   a starving

infant squalling.   And once, full
stop: precipiced, crescendoed rush

of water that never stops falling.

Exodus in X Minor

My grandmother, bed-ridden, bled
from her kidneys, her brain, and the skin
beneath my nails began to blue
chronically. I streamed hot
water over them, transient
fix. We marveled at the bruising
balls of ice our lawn collected, felt
thunder through the porch beams
where we sat watching fire branch
in the sky, Lord, in the sky
and somehow light nothing. Our street
began harvesting mattresses
curbside, our neighbors shielding
their rashed arms & legs, bitten
by insects that moved like apple
seeds tossed in a breeze. I hummed
          will the circle
                    be unbroken
under my breath for weeks. I cut
the tips from my gloves, the better
to wear them always. We sipped
our whiskey & the cracked glasses
held. We took a pup the breeder couldn't sell
          by and by, Lord, by and by
we fed her, blanket-wrapped. She nosed
my shoulder until she fell asleep. We woke
to find her dead. We named her

Whiskey. My nails purpled. My red-
bearded man took to the woods for several days
and nights, barrels
loaded for deer. He returned carrying
nothing but purple
winter roses. *I'll forge you*
a blade, he said. *We'll call it your*
fox tongue. He held my
          hands in his, and they felt him.

Erzsébet Báthory Shows the Fox-Haired Seer How She Was Forced to Watch Her Teenage Lover's Execution, Then Sequestered for Nine Months Until Her Infant Daughter Was Taken from Her at Birth

he was my one   pure

carried me

flowers

to bed

away

to the window

to watch him torn

to listen   the dogs

to a hazier

hazier

God

& back

Lucifer's clear yard of a world

to the never
looking away to the looking

glass   to
brush

my own white face   my own bitten

lips   my own dark   hair my   own darkened eyes   my own dark   now

Mine

Magdalena's Husband Burned Down Their Apartment Building When His Meth Lab Caught Fire, and Her Lover Shot Himself to Death in Front of Her and Her Three Small Children Two Months Later

last moments   before you   open the door   know it will
hurt   children assembled   lover cowering   eyes small dishes whose
low centers have   gathered   loose   drops   It will hurt   this   opening
your   skull with bullets   your heart   won't stop right away

Tarnish-free   is a promise   you're ready   to cash in on

three children   clustered   on her lap   she tries   to keep them & they try
not to move   she might   be speaking   you   are ready

to open that door   & not be sorry
again   her voice   familiar   white rush   & just enough   impurity
enough

empty   after   in which the right thing is a drab
damp bundle of twigs that won't light   in the low   center of calm

the knob in your hand

is ready to snap shut & open you open you open

yes yes yes yes yes

Letter to Diane Arbus

Blessed are those

among us able learn a few new

walls out of all the surrounding

buildings housing strangers: that is to say, bodies

and the time they give us.

Or: Stepping over purple-eyed

prostrates, the hotel a kaleidoscope

of verdigris & gangrene.

Top floor, a many-pillowed

human cloaked & preening

in estrogen

& negligee—

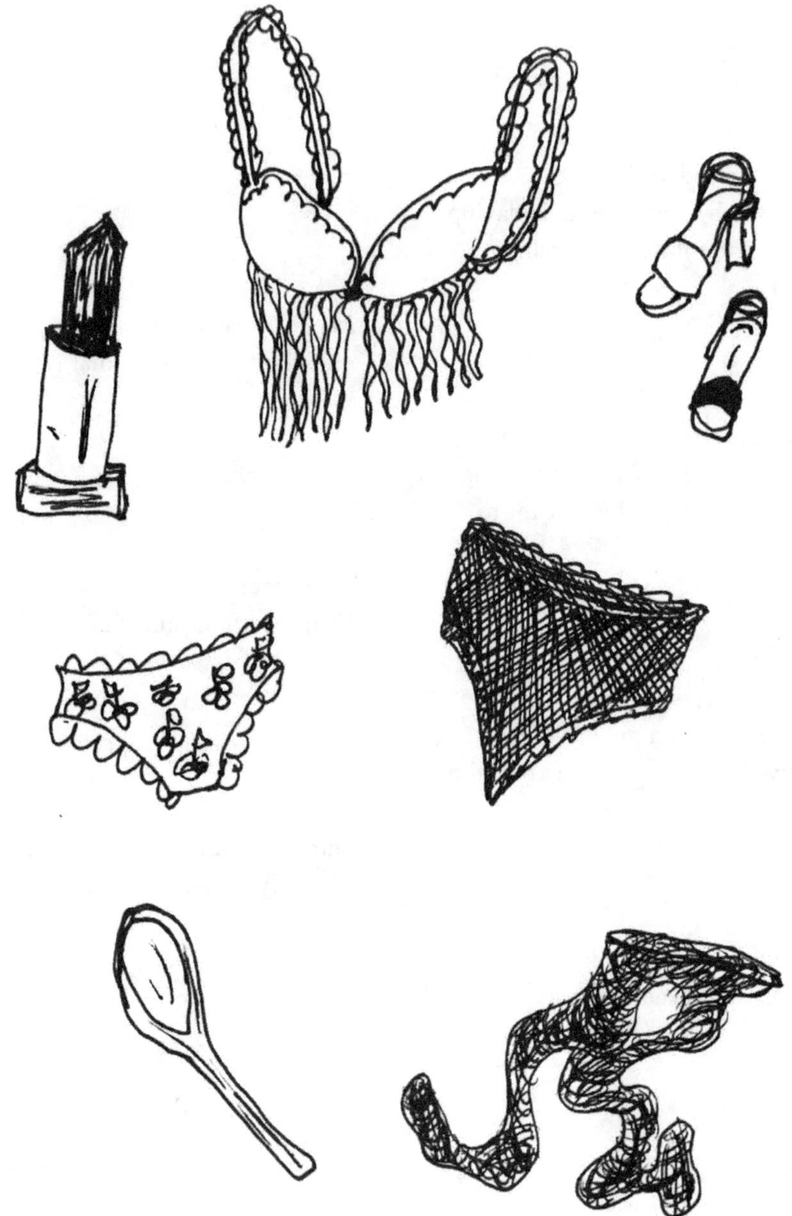

Exodus in X Minor

our streets grew red with men
          painted by vernal cold, behaving
                    as ibises   searching

My red-bearded man knew a hill,
one night dug a hole that guided

for serpents, bare-toothed & welcoming
          storm winds   the rivers rising as
                    though they meant to come for us

blood into the soft earth.
I woke to find him staring.

and did   the waters browned
          what had been green
     swallowed   one poxed bird

Our sheets a muddied shroud:
The only woman who knows

spread her wings   exposed
          garish plumage   treacly
                    feathers gaping   body

me, he said   threw a bottle
of whiskey   my way   chased

sored   floated & eyed
the red in his beard
wood piled with bodies

it with wine   screamed, *Get out*
of my house   the doorway

drifted past   the waters moved
the waters left us   having claimed
their tithe   our steps grew

stained red for weeks   He
dreamed so hard of eyes

red with her: I had
drawn the blade he forged me
and knew it was mine.

that never closed: I saw them
I saw with them.

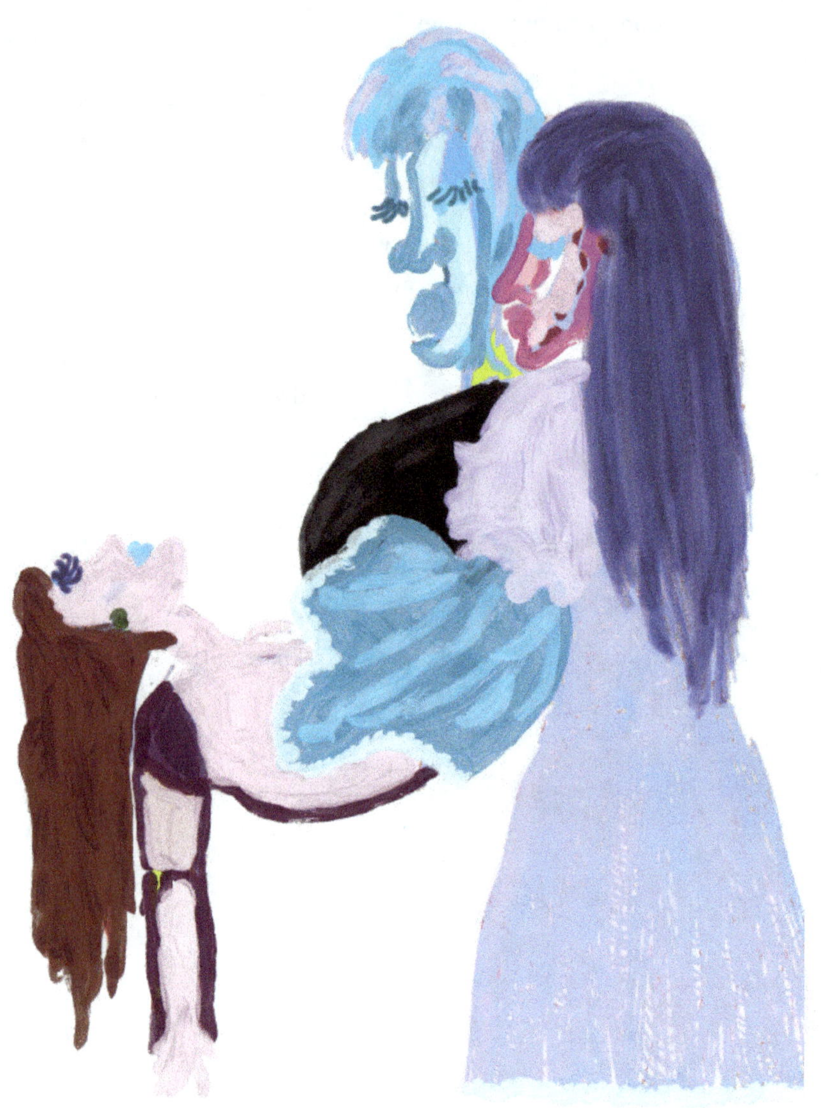

Erzsébet Báthory Explains to the Fox-Haired Seer How She Began to Administer Increasingly Harsh Punishments for Any Transgressions, Treating Each as a Brazen Affront to Her Authority, and Developed an Aptitude for Power

and gasping wildly
yes

self-preservation a severe & austere art I find
myself fairer with each artery cut

severed / as ever: graced

bodies curve & splay
what sprays saved Never so much

as a bath my bright

alabaster basin another stained
serf my shadow my touch my

transforming erase:

they are voided made my own

skin
polished, luminous
as a hollowed bone

fair as a duckling's
first sticky

down
down my *yes*

the first
fat & lasting

flake caught by a cold
& welcoming tongue

Last Time I Got Tattooed, Two Men Sat in the Shop Hypothesizing Aloud About Why Women Frequently Return to Men Who Abuse Them, Ultimately Concluding in Consensus that Women Enjoy Being Assaulted by Men

For Saumya and Sammie

My grandmother lived alone in the country at eighty on a ninety-acre farm
that was more wilderness than farm at that point and she slept with a carriage

gun under her bed.   She with her blue eyes taught me to respect guns
and women with guns   if not women   my mother   with her

blue eyes taught me to straighten my untamable mane to lower my voice to use
my dark eyes appropriately   lowered like my voice   saying please

and thank you as in   Please
don't   Please   stop doing that   please   stop

I grew older   I had boyfriends and other
men who taught me   what happens

to quiet pretty   or quiet not pretty
enough   please stop

The day Hillary Clinton was elected 45th President of the United States of
America   by the people of the United States of America   she lost to

I spent that day in a strip club. The kind that only serves soda and does full
nudity before noon.   I was there to interview some of the dancers
in the morning. I had to use the bathroom and there were eight dancers, Juicy-
clad looking relaxed and laughing in their sweatsuits and thongs backstage
which is where the bathroom was   and the stall door was nonexistent
and they didn't seem to mind at all which sort of made sense when I
                                                                    thought about it
a couple of the bouncers came back and they were teasing one about
how he was getting married next month but in a way where really they were
celebrating him and complimenting his fiancée
and then in the main area of the club there were these men that I still

all these months later I still can't describe or breathe when I try to describe them

          and one of the dancers came up to me and asked if she could give me a
private dance and I was caught off-guard
(because she knew I was there to talk with her, and her colleagues,
to listen to their stories about taking the clubs to court and winning
recognition as private contractors who could set their own hours, their own rules,
                                                   and not there to receive private dances?)
and I said no thank you and she took my hands and asked if I was *sure she
couldn't*
          and I said no thank you and she released my hands and slinked across
the club to one of the men   and I realized   I couldn't breathe
                    and then I felt like an idiot for not saying yes but it was too late

     and then I went to vote
               and then I went home and watched her be elected by the people
     and my violent then-husband fell asleep and when he woke up he said
       Madame President? and I said no   and he said but that's impossible
and it's hard for me to put this into a poem because I refuse to render in beautiful
language all the things that happened in the days after that

and some of my friends and I kept joking, during those days, about getting IUDs and guns but then all five of us actually went out and took the tests and did the paperwork and waited the necessary number of days while someones checked our backgrounds

and a few days later a white lady in a Ralph Lauren sweater interrupted me while I was speaking to one of my friends to tell me that *more guns are never the answer* and asked me whether I had tried meditating or singing to focus on my light

and when I say it's difficult to put this in a poem and when I say I find myself
resisting the impulse to render this in language that will dizzy
or swoon or seduce you what I'm trying to say is

bother me in the street today & I'll scream
it won't be for help

one of my ex-husbands who assaulted me taught me the exact
spot on the bridge

of your nose to smash with my forehead
like a soccer ball I'm not obligated

to explain shit to my grandmother taught me
how to shoot & I guess really what she taught me is that I like guns

hot noise that makes you feel
as though you yourself are popping open falling gold ammunition's tiny weight

variations
the choreography of all the safety rules not unlike an archaic etiquette manual

intended to keep you alive. The aesthetic: barrel, cylinder, hammer
grip & sight. The simplicity of my body is not contestable territory

because I say it's not.   Maybe there's a reason we're told to shun
          that which makes us dangerous   to those who would

                                                        There was a time when I resisted
these lessons: cried & tried   so hard to figure out

how to make myself acceptably cute inside of them (*I mean, with your ethnic nose, cute is the best you can hope for. The best you can hope for,*

                                        said someone I loved before I had surgery
                              to look more like all the women in my life who are

just being honest).   I want to refuse
to straighten or stain my raven & silver hair any more let the dark & glittering

plumage crown me   thrash from my scalp
                    thrive in their wild   gyrate defiance

But I am afraid   of things that have already been said to me
or done to me   my eyes are blue now and my hair is auburn

                                        I love how I look and I hate
                                                  & don't hate that I adapted to
                                            please stop   please

I believe that a gun is a spiritual weapon.   I am a spiritual

weapon.   I paint

my skin from the inside   needle it to bleeding
plumage that heals brightly but never   stops keening   *please   please*

motherfucker   please   try   to stop
me   from howling down what's mine

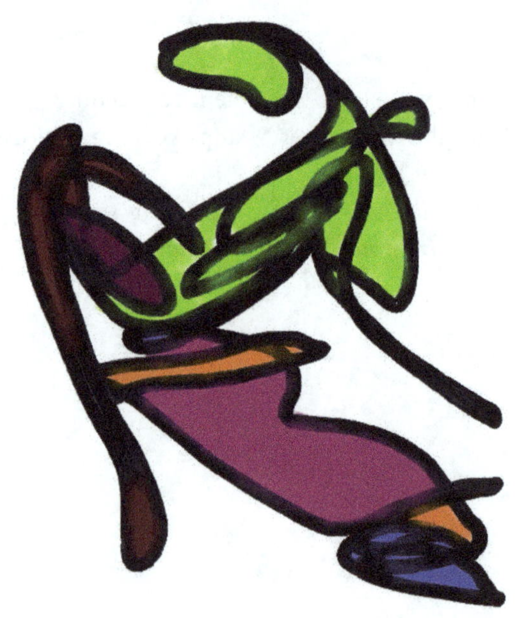

Everywhere in the World, They Hurt Little Girls

The year after I was born, a girl named Cheri in the vampire
town where we both lived got her first paper route.
Cheri wanted to earn enough money to throw
her pregnant middle school teacher a baby shower. Cheri took

over the neighborhood paper route from James,
a middle-aged neighbor. Every day after school, Cheri delivered
her entire neighborhood their *Evening Star*.
Her mother usually accompanied Cheri to collect

payments, but one day it happened that James
was a week overdue on his subscription, and her mother
had to get dinner started, so Cheri went
unescorted to James' house, which is when James pulled her

right off the front steps and locked her inside his house
with him, and hurt her, because James is a man
who likes hurting little girls. He made Cheri
bleed, made her cry, made her feel terrorized

and alone. Then, James made her go
missing. I don't want to say he brought her
life to an end. Partly because her memory lives
through the park that the city named after her,

and because her spirit lives, too. I believe that we are
made of gossamer, crystalline, infinite, shimmering
material inside ourselves and the things our bodies do.
But also, I don't want to say he killed her because it's obscene

to announce that he did it, that men like James do
exactly what they want in this world, make the horror stick. Sick.
Thirty-four years later, Cheri's mother keeps her daughter's
bedroom exactly the same: her clarinet, her emerald green Girl

Scout sash, her catcher's mitt, the decorative throw
pillows that Cheri had made herself. Cheri's mother
has been wearing the same pair of earrings
for the past thirty-four years. These earrings are special

because Cheri was wearing them when she was taken
away from her mother for the rest of this life.
When Cheri's body was found, the earrings remained
missing. Someone had removed them. A trophy

later recovered from the bowels of James' house.
Cheri's mother took them, the last thing to touch her child's body,
and inserted them into her own. Posted in her lobes. I am thirty-six years old
when I first learn of all this, reading about the park where I used to take

my dog when I lived in this vampiric little town. The park named for
little Cheri Lindsey, whose bedroom has never changed in all these
years.   I am breastfeeding my newborn daughter   as I read about Cheri,

who was raped   and murdered   for trying   to celebrate   a baby being born,
and a woman becoming   a new mother.   I am
living in California, where

there are birds of paradise   pools of flawless   tumbled aquamarine
water, each wave
in the pool a glittering
facet of precious stone, and pomegranate & avocado

& lemon trees & so many orange trees up north
that you can smell them when you drive up the Pacific Coast Highway, even if you
keep all your windows closed. But I am back
in that town I was born into, which I hated because it was filled

with vampires, remembering how locals pronounced the name
of her memorial park: *Cherry*.
My daughter has
had difficulty latching. I accept full responsibility for this,

because a baby
cannot fail her mother it's not possible. I hate my body for failing
my little star however it's failing her, and I cry
frequently because I don't

understand exactly *how* I'm failing her what's wrong
with my body or me, why I can't
do better in giving my daughter
what she needs but today as I'm reading this bottomless

horror, my daughter latches and I have to hold my breath
afraid that if I cry she will lose her latch, lose her chance
to draw strength and health from my body into hers, shockingly
painful sacrament shared between us. I'm so thankful

now that she's gnawing on me that she doesn't have teeth I sneeze once
and she begins to wail furiously her rage delights me, is welcome
relief we are at home in Southern California's
Shadow Hills, which everyone knows are haunted air acrid with smoke

this morning, another wildfire they're not even scary anymore
most of the time just hard to breathe in real California palms
flutter over the balcony Peacocks roam the suburban streets freely
dragging their ardent, amorous tails like regal

medieval hems through the dust   their forebears escaped
from Patrick Swayze's ranch   decades ago   mated
populating the hills with their   aggressive beauty
our palms   flutter with increasing fervor   these breezes

cold & sweet
delicious, comforting
reminder that someone
loves us all,

but in reality, high winds
mean that the fires will spread
ever more quickly, today. I skim
news reports for evacuation orders

.

& there aren't any. Yet. At least,
not for us. The sky is still paradise
blue over one side of the house.
I don't believe that things will get better.

Teresa Was One of Four Catholic Workers in Ithaca, New York, Who Spilled Her Blood at a Military Recruitment Center in Protest of the USA's Invasion of Iraq, and Was Subsequently Arrested and Imprisoned

sweet anaerobic
frenzy   gilded

point each volant
contraction

can't remove

syntactic fantastic
synaptic collapse

happy apathy
slap of apnea

tactile epiphany
oxidizing lakeful red

more more more more
red

The Fox-Haired Seer Walks Barefoot to the Rivers and Is Baptized, as the Water Itself Embraces Her and Sings Her the Parable of Confluence

I let the current have me. My fox
watched from riverbank. I told myself

it was   my blood he wanted   my feet cut
by the trek.   I walked until I did not care where I bled

out. These waters   known as ruthless, returned
trespassers to surface   melted, skeletal. Cruel basin

of rain & death   unyielding floes usurping
whatever fell into their   windchilled crucible.

I let myself fall   because I had walked to the water.
I let myself walk there before I could   walk no longer.

I put my mouth to its nebulous
surface, said, *My body*

is your body   and I was
under.   Beneath its burnished hazel,

I saw lesions   lacerations   torturous
abrasions   what life it had sustained   razed to full

fathomed hell   plastics   toxic metals   layered chemical
grime.   Piscine, amphibian   animals writhed.   *My body*

is your body, the confluence sang back, *scarred*
detritus in the world of men. I dimmed & didn't

mind.   Through a bed of sorrel
blossoms, my fox trailed   silent.

Overhead, distant   calls of raven
followed me down   *Your secret*

doorway is a gift.   Enraged, I felt
my pulse jab brighter, spiralling   in a flush

onyx blue-lit feathers falling   soft against my scalp
What downy grift is this? My body

is no courier   is of no consequence
my mouth is allowed to   glitter, narcissine

& wet   abject   with desire,   or fold
itself shut   silent and serene

But you are not to bend the knee obsidian-eyed glisten
and you are not a queen   stand again &   step   into your worth

Cold & heavy fluid velvet
rocked me   chastened, christened   split the earth   & keened:

You will learn to speak until they listen.
You will tell them all that you have seen.

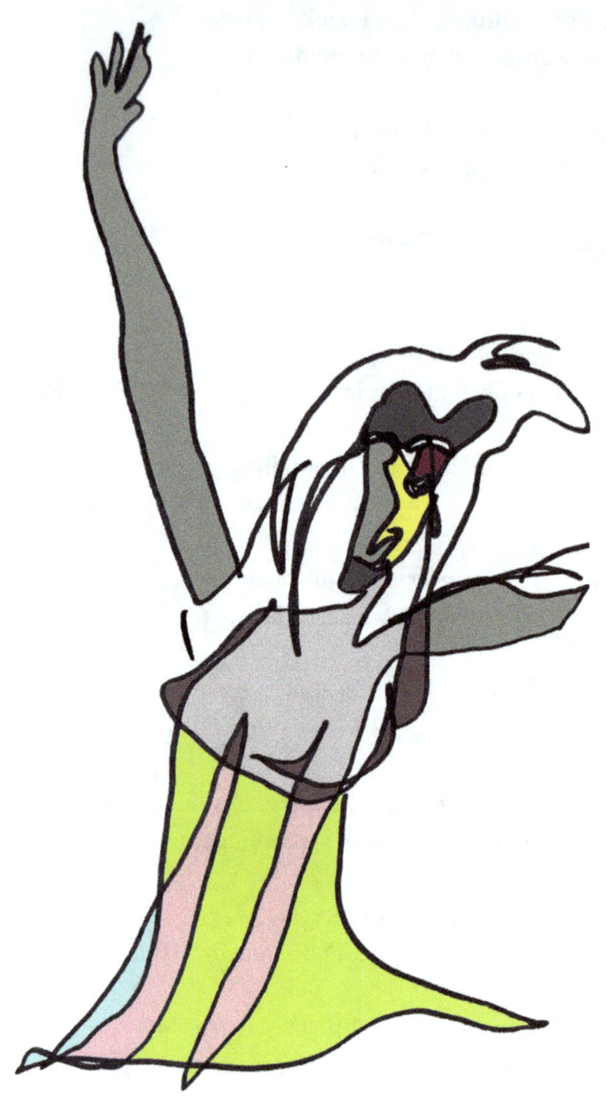

Exodus in X Minor

The bodies piled in our hot cellar:
black-and-yellow pebbles ambering
    in humid air.   I gasped

each time I saw them. Community
gardens closed, parks nursed
suffering baby oaks as a mother

struggling for her children. Frogs
stormed our cellar, declaring *one*
    by one   *we'll gain the portals*

with a shock of teeth. I moved
my paintings from our basement
mausoleum of translucent, silenced

wings.   Our tall field's fireflies
never appeared again   *there to dwell*
    with the immortals   My red-bearded

man sailed the rivers to
their confluence on a ram-
shackle raft: it capsized

twice before he finally swam
    ashore   *that land*
beyond the river,   arrived

home & held me   against his nude
  Celtic ink: my throat
    swelled shut.   I wheezed for   weeks

  at his skin.   I took my paintings
from the walls.   I learned to squeeze
  my blade so that no   blood would come.

I held its handle. I rolled my
wrist under its weight. I held
my breath.   I counted.

Erzsébet Báthory Shows the Fox-Haired Seer the Letter in Which She Wrote, "You Will Find a Man in Me," to One of Her Trespassers, Even as She Interceded on Behalf of Other Women, Including Assault Victims

noble the stubborn
horse collapsed but will
when whipped rise & run again

lovely the punch
-yellow petals converting to cloud & burst
out in a dance of breath enviable
finale of further beget

as a child, I held her
many carved faces red-clad onyx-faired
each body pregnant with another

I am the noblest
blow: bearing final
peace the deepest

felt frost settling
ground to its true
barren brown Inside

my smallest
doll's belly: a bullet
plump as spring.
I am the barrel

through which it screams
once. The quickest
click bend. I am the powder
& furnace that forges
the smoke of your
          hot metal end.

Stranded in Rural Upstate New York, the Fox-Haired Seer Walks Miles to the Nearest Building, A Small Abattoir, Seeking Relief from the Elements

Her twin waits, throat-splayed,

hapless on the hosed concrete.
          A fresh knife sharpening

jingles, insouciant Hooks,

pullied, hang the beauty
higher as he strips the canvas

thick balloon of

hide from the body.
The floor mixes

into marble: her face freed

of its fluids, her eyes
bright as a mime's, naked

legs pieced in graceful

jerks, the skin-
 less wound still

flowing, broochlike, the dark

size of a bauble. The true
belly, already wheel-

barrowed, swells in

this heat. They're known
to explode, these summers,

but no one steps away.

Letter to Diane Arbus

these cushions fatten

us: twisting, contorted

finding

some new

way to become

(weathered, Other)

I mean my coat

of human

My zipper.

Exodus in X Minor

finally sped West together letters that followed us read
wash out all the violet
you'd like to we remember you when the fire

gutted downtown you when a man stormed Main Street with aristocratic steel blade hacking limbs from strangers you when the gorges froze and kept flood waters in our streets you when we know we'll

disappear my pocketed fox tongue
hummed like an extracted
heart: the thrill

of cleaving had left me
wanting more than dove or lamb

or Fox: horizon like sweet cold razing
liquid or a wristed razor. Beyond. Be-
yonder

we saw aubrenwing lilaced by evening
climbed like viola strains into the air
we escaped we were
escaping one carved

tree trunk at a time towards our Croatoan

not being but becoming

creatures newer more brightly made

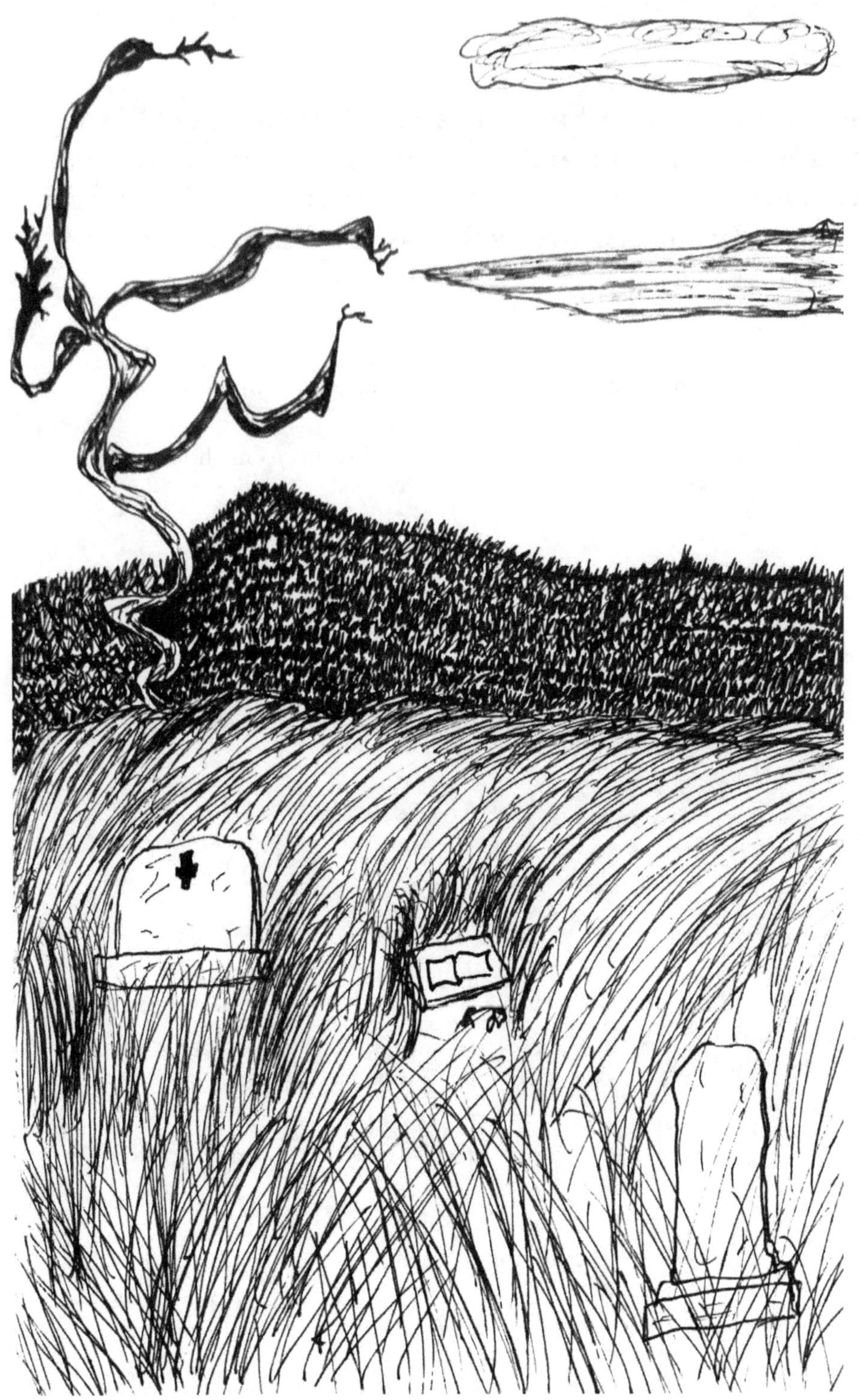

Erzsébet Báthory Shows the Fox-Haired Seer How She Was Barred from Attending Her Own Trial, Was Convicted in Nonconsensual Absentia, and Ultimately Walled Inside a Series of Rooms for Years Until Her Death

one stone &another winter

air spiked grey by breath / my heart:

sparrows over slate-iced lake

beneath leaden sky. Each

page less

legible my fine

dress torn toneless. What

dusted heather: each colder

finger folding in desperate

unwilled prayer each greying

nail one small

stone and then another

The Fox-Haired Seer Reads New Research in Which Scientists Causally Link Early Salivary Glands with What Eventually Became Venom Glands in Many Animals, Suggesting that Humans May Someday Evolve to Become Venomous

In the dawn of those contagion years, we didn't
know whether we passed death

by our breath, living plane

to plane country to country to crowded

funerary ceremonies
synchronicities spanning

oceans. But we knew our bodies

hosts for this disease
breeding

colonies of virus writhing to invade as in one

dusky vampire town where one

sick asymptomatic

man broke all shelter

in place orders & crept to city center. Spit.

& again & again
into his palms like self-stigmata

anointed

door handles parked cars essential shops service bells at pharmacies
medicinal lids traffic-signal push-plates knobs on office doors the errant
unfortunate street lamp elevator buttons
railings on stairways escalators mezzanines & then delicious

wait:

how many bodies touched by blight

nurtured & birthed

by his? Remember your last knock
on the street—

spike in the sidewalk, rushing passerby's
hurried push. Remember your body

feel the coming plummet   suspended   swaying

you think
I could fall right now, and then you sink

through air the flail the reach

the moment after, when you thank your stars
steadied by anonymous

communal surface, heart beating prayer

of gratitude for injury avoided whatever solid

communal object onto which you've just laid hands

unguarded

Peter Was One of Four Catholic Workers in Ithaca, New York, Who Spilled His Blood at a Military Recruitment Center to Protest the USA's Invasion of Iraq, and Was Subsequently Arrested and Imprisoned

strangle makes a minute

oubliette   forgetting

is the war

These are waterless springs and mists driven by storm. The greatest darkness has been reserved for them.

soldier's skull halved like melon & filled by time with rainwater   I could

drink it   I'm a razor blade

now   no aphagia   emulous

timorous   tremulous

The dog laps its own vomit. The sow is bathed only
to wallow again in mud.

The earth was first formed in

There, there

is Atlantis.

water; the world of that time was deluged with water and perished. The present world and heavens have

ubiquitous

obsequies

what fraught

requiem

been reserved for fire. They shall be kept until the day of judgment's destruction of the godless.

The Fox-Haired Seer, Whose Raven Roots Have Asserted Themselves While Her Daughter Grows Inside Her Belly, Reads of a Murder Just Outside Her Hometown and, Muscles Contracting, Considers the Parable of Pink

The summer I became pregnant with my daughter,
an eleven-year-old girl in upstate New York named
Jacelyn was murdered. Jacelyn had two half-
brothers; they all shared the same birth mother,
though Jacelyn had not seen her biological mother in
years, had been raised by her custodial mother since
eighteen months of age. Jacelyn frequently went with
her brothers to visit their father, James. All of them stayed in
James' trailer, where his boyfriend of eighteen years,
Toby, also resided. Jacelyn's favorite colors were red
and pink. She often stopped by the classroom of the
woman who had been her kindergarten teacher,
offering to help with classroom chores at the end
of the day. Jacelyn's town of 600 people turned out
wearing red and pink, carrying candles, walking to
her elementary school after the news broke
regarding her death, and the torture she endured
before she died. Watching the mass of pink and red,
I thought of all the baby clothes friends had sent
for my unborn daughter, wondered if she, too,
might favor pink, whether that would change as
she grew up. I thought about telling her how my
own favorites are silver, red, and purple, but how
hot pink was my longtime favorite, how pink in the
early 16th century meant to pierce or stab someone
with a weapon or a missile; how it later meant to stab
or pierce at all, or simply to cut a saw-toothed edge on

something. A hundred years later, finally, it came to
mean the flower of the plant we call pink, for its
jagged edges. And only fifty years after that, it became
the color pink as we know it, but also the color red—for example,
men who hunted foxes wore red clothing called hunting pinks.
And pink was, for the next hundred years, considered a color
intended for men. The color of carnage, blood, passion, fury.
Little men, little lords swathed in pink those first moments
after birth, red faces screaming like oracles exactly who they'd be
raised into. And in the 1940s, Macy's finally won the commercial
color wars, and pink became the color for girls; boys wanted nothing
to do with it, soon after, and Jacelyn probably wouldn't have
cared about any of this. She died of asphyxiation, but also suffered
blunt-force trauma to the head, and hemorrhaged. She died
while resisting the sexual assault that Toby's DNA would later prove he committed,
although the father of her brothers, James, is believed by investigators
to have participated in Jacelyn's murder and assault, as well. James immediately
lied to police, suggesting his own sons, Jacelyn's brothers,
were the likely perpetrators, "based on their mindset," he said,
but refused to elaborate further. Toby refused
to speak in court—not to apologize,
not to express remorse, not even to offer any
explanation or motivation for having tortured a child.
I breathe in, and my daughter kicks, spinning.
The hills are beginning to brighten, late September
monarchs fluttering through scarlet leaves.
I've been thinking of names, lately.
Just yesterday, I learned Jacelyn
means, "Supplanter," or
"One who conquers,"
or, in some translations,
"One who is protected by God."

A Spiritualist Medium, A Priestess of Lucumí, and A Devotee of Santísima Muerte All Individually Deliver Messages to the Fox-Haired Seer that Her Red-Bearded Man Will Soon Kill Her If She Does Not Leave Him

When I was four, I drowned for the first time. Ensconced in aquamarine
current scented like chemical burns, knew I had been through

this portal before. And would again. The world mirror-
balled into blackness. *Bhrúigh*

m'athair mo chroí le buille arís. Reborn, blurring back
into a world so bright it hurt to see, I could see

all the sacred silver threads that web the world. Fifteen years later,
I slid, slender silver thread unanchored, through frozen winter

pond. Under the doctor's burning gentle hand, I dreamed myself
at thirty-six. The children I would leave behind. At thirty-three,

I told my red-bearded husband—*Is eagal liom go bhfuil trí bliana*
fágtha agam le maireachtáil. Would he be the one to catch and

breathe me back? But his body in the end was the very pool of viscous
that filled my lungs, that fluid weight and wait each

time I tried to cry for help. *Lig dom tú a dhéanamh torrach,*
he said, my shoulder bruise still fresh. *Tá a fhios agam gur*

tusa mo thodhchaí. I felt it: he wanted to cradle & press my last
breath inside his fist. One night in his forest cabin, built

on my river's edge, I dreamed he held me beneath the waters
while my daughter clung to my hands, my unborn son

somehow still screamed my name. I forced myself to push her
hands away so I would not pull her under with me. The next time

he staggered drunk and angry into my father's house, I said, *You have*
to leave. I wept until my body had no choice but

sleep. *Caithfidh tú imeacht.* I dipped below the waves, welcoming cold
oblivion, cradled my daughter to my core. She held my

hand even as I dipped below. I pulled us both to safety at the obsidian
bottom of that tossing ocean. We encountered gods like moons

among goddesses like planets. Ancestors in constellation, mingling.
There is nothing further I can tell you: I saw his death, a single

bleeding tree
among so many trees.

Then ricocheted, jagged star, through sable
portal dreamworlds into this. M*á tá teachtaireacht*

ag duine ar bith le seoladh,
bheadh tú ciallmhar a rá liom anois—

Exodus in X Minor

A man was arrested on Front Street, drunk,
for shooting strangers with a bow and arrow.
A projectile intended for practice becomes
something else when you put it through a human.

There was meth in my in-laws' house, and cocaine
in little bags. People falling down the stairs in dead
of night. They grew their own weed to save
money, and everyone swam along, poured spirits
down their throats, bottles upon bottles nightly; spirits
hung from the ceiling like mildewed barn tarps
or decaying cloth diapers. They pulled at my hair
each time I passed beneath. Money went missing—dropped
on the carpet, laid on the bureau, folded inside a wallet. It didn't

matter where, because
                    no place was safe.   A lockbox

was what my spouse suggested. The theft couldn't be
stopped without security. A system. A lock-
box, airtight, light-devouring, static, stubborn, secure
becomes something else when sealed around
a human core. *I dreamed you were a witch,* he said,

laughed until I felt cold, told
myself it was only whiskey making him
this way   again: *You ate some poison*
plants from your stupid fucking garden that you

wasted all our money on, so I
cremated you. Burned your body
while you died.

I woke the next morning to a blight on my garden, mutated
microscopic insect that resisted every kind of poison
the professionals suggested. I found condoms

that weren't ours, hidden in the dresser drawer. I held them
out for him to see and he said, *How long have you been having these*
persistent   disturbing   thoughts?

Maybe you should   see someone
You're scaring me.

Within three days, all of my garden had died. He suggested
that I burn the remains. A spouse transforms into

something else after he fucks other women, but
still something else after he threatens to kill you.

A spouse becomes something
else after he works

up the nerve to mean it.

The Fox-Haired Seer, in a Moment of Deep Despair, Comes to Understand the Parable of the Healer and the Dark Grey Cat

I was riding the city bus and crying silently because my friend Valentine had killed herself. She had been missing for days before the police found her body. The bus reached my stop. As tears blurred my vision, I didn't realize that the mechanism used to lower the bus steps was malfunctioning. I fell several feet to the ground, and didn't really grasp what was happening until I hit the pavement.

Everything I was carrying with me went flying out of my hands. The items in my tote bag were knocked out, rolling into the street. The fall was so bad it tore my skirt. I had cuts and scrapes on my knees, legs, hands, and arms. I did my best not to burst into tears, which, since I was already crying, was more of a challenge than it might otherwise have been.

This tiny, dainty woman with wild curls appeared seamlessly in front of me. She had somehow gathered all my things and put them back into my bag. She wordlessly put the bag over her shoulder, and without warning she put her hands on me. Instinctively, I resisted—I hate being touched by strangers. I physically recoiled, I grabbed her hands and threw them back at her, and finally I pushed her shoulders to move her out of my space. She ignored my resistance. She picked me up and lifted me into the air, then set me down on my feet.

I was stunned from the fall, and stunned by the news of Valentine's death; but I was also stunned by this woman's ability to lift me, and the fact that she didn't seem to even register my resistance. So I didn't resist when she half-lifted me onto her other shoulder (the one not holding my bag), and placed me on a nearby bench. She dropped the bag at my feet.

"Thank you," I said uncomfortably, and reached for the bag.

She made a wordless gesture that amounted to, "Leave your bag alone."

She brought out these odd, colorful little jars from her pockets and opened them, then smeared some sort of herbal unguents on my scrapes and cuts. She put a dab of something on my head. I really hate being touched on my head, even by people I'm close to; I always have. But at this point, I was filled with a kind of wonder. I didn't want to stop her.

"I didn't hit my head," I said, though I already, somehow, knew.

She looked at me, evaluating, then dipped a finger into another of the bright jars and added some other substance to my scalp. I couldn't think of anything else to say, so I sat there silently. Something inside me shifted. I wanted to burst into tears again, but this time the way you cry when you feel safe.

The woman leaned in close, almost right up against me, and rubbed my limbs quickly all over, one at a time. Then all of them again.

"Thank you," I said again. This time, I meant it. I didn't know what was different, but I could feel that something had changed.

She took hold of both my arms and squeezed, like she was bracing me for something.

"Thank you," I said again. "I'm all right now. Thank you."

She nodded and stepped back. I bent down to pick up my bag, then stood—intending to hug her, to thank her properly, to apologize for having pushed her away so hard. But she was gone.

Ten years later, I would dream of this woman, on the final night of a nine-day novena I'd prayed to St. Jude, pleading for my then-husband to be guided into rehab. I knew that he had been unfaithful in our marriage, had threatened me, had harmed me; but I desperately believed that if he entered treatment & recovery, he would become the man he'd convinced me he once was. That morning, I awoke to find that he had stolen the money we'd earmarked for baby gates out of my bank account and used it to pay for a year's subscription to Tinder Gold. I had a panic attack, chest pains. Struggled to breathe. Thoroughly jarred from dreamworlds, I forgot the healer with the wild curls.

Later that morning, as I drove home alone from my divorce lawyer's office, the dream came flowing softly back to me. I remembered her green trousers, her dark hair, delicate bone structure. How on earth did she lift me into the air? And then, as the memory passed over me like a comforting fog, a dark-grey cat ran like a puma in front of my car, up ahead on the road.

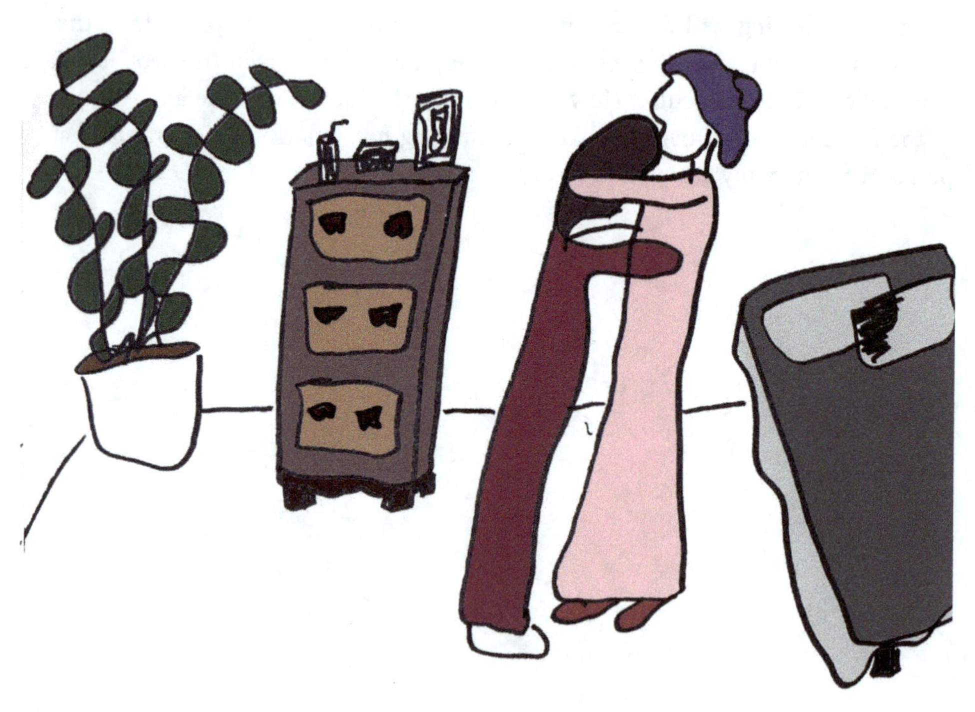

Erzsébet Báthory Draws the Fox-Haired Seer a Bath, Strikes Up A Nocturne, and Slips Into the Water Beside Her

I find myself.   Invited: sliding your dark
locks   nape to collar-
bone, bare

shoulder a lake
blanketed in early
snow   & those   blue

threads laced   racing
fluid beneath luminescent
translucence

slash is uncomely crime, gash   common-torn
grime.   *Slit*, that's
better-brushed   *slice*

is sweet   *slide*   see how it
flows   soaring from you like one
unbounded

unfolding   underwater
wing   & nothing
so endless   comforting   as   *me*   sliding

in   to   *you*

The Fox-Haired Seer Visits the Abandoned NXIVM Headquarters in Albany, NY, and Reflects that Perhaps Cults Have Historically Been Associated with "Devil Worship" Because the Men Who Rule Over Them Are Demons Made Flesh

In the beginning, there was a man who earned your faith and by this I mean he made you believe.   He was like the strong man in ancient scripts who felled kings and divided their spoils. He would hold you. He would hold all the places where someone else had cut holes into you; and you knew he could heal you. See how he cast out demons from the spaces other people had cut into you, had cut you away to give the demons entry. If you're honest: in the beginning were your wounds, gasps like words.   The strong man tells you the truth is like a mustard seed. He puts one inside a glass bead: bids you wear it. You do, to please him, around your throat. He teaches you to visualize it while you meditate, to perfect your vision of the massive tree you will grow if you accept his seed, nurture it inside yourself. Soon, you can see the tree without his voice on the back of your neck, without even closing your eyes. You understand now: the tree has always existed. You were wrong when you didn't know you had climbed it as a child, swung from it on a tire, carved your initials into its base.

Once you have cultivated this tree, the man helps you understand how beauty is like leaven, you like the wife who took some leaven and hid it in three measures of flour. By morning, all of the flour was leavened. Transformed.   You are the wife, and you are also the flour. You are beautiful, to him if no one else, and now you must accept his beauty into yourself as well. As he envelops you. You tell him shyly that the word *envelops* always reminds you of the canyon you drove through, alone, post-wildfire. Ash heavy in the air, in your lungs, the trees charred to something you couldn't name. Embarrassed, you say tentatively, *I felt so badly for the trees.*   He holds your gaze and nods, and says, *But you must stop that feeling. Their destruction was a religious experience for them. All those decades of slow growth, and then suddenly, like lightning, they were consumed.   Enveloped.* Transformed into new information. You understand that the first sparks are like leavening, the canyon of trees like the flour. You are chosen by this strong man: he admires your spark. But it must be nurtured into something larger. He is here to help you learn to envy those trees. They have always been burned, have always been burning, were always intended to burn. They grew, yes, but they were also grown. Grown so that someday they might be burned.

The strong man loves you. You wish you could touch a part of him that you've never seen, the part where there's a void, the part you could heal with your love, mortar his wounds with gold dust lacquer like a precious vase, because you love him very deeply. You try to explain this to him, but he interrupts to tell you love is actually more like the glass bead that holds the mustard seed. Not a gilded unguent, but a large glass jar: airtight, created by the same lightning that set your tree alight, by striking sand. This flawless artifact is filled with cornmeal, and the cornmeal is love, and you must carry this vessel home from the market. You don't notice anything wrong as you carefully bear it home in your arms; no accidents, no mistakes you can discern. You're filled with care. But when you reach home, the jar is empty. When did you cause the first break? Why weren't you more attentive? The cornmeal—scattered to the winds, irrevocably. How can love be both lightning and cornmeal? A glass bead, a jar, a seed, a burning tree? Why did you think it was gold dust? Where is each grain now? All the sounds of a gathering summer storm. Winds intensify, the mustard tree sways in your vision. When did your tree catch fire? Did it burn, or is it still standing? Was everything starry, when lightning struck? Was your body the tree, or attached to the tree with iron spikes? Or was it pierced, cracking like a spiderweb? Were you enveloped in his love, or did you toss it away? Where will you go when you are released back into the bright waters at the edges of the universe? What sounds do you make when you shatter? Are they lost in the screams of the wind? You can see the tree, and the ash, glass shards, cornmeal floating like lost stars. The strong man takes your face in both his hands, a tender gesture: he lifts your trembling chin, steadies you with his eyes.   Will you believe what you see, or what he can see here? What he works so hard to show you? All this truth. All this beauty. So much love.

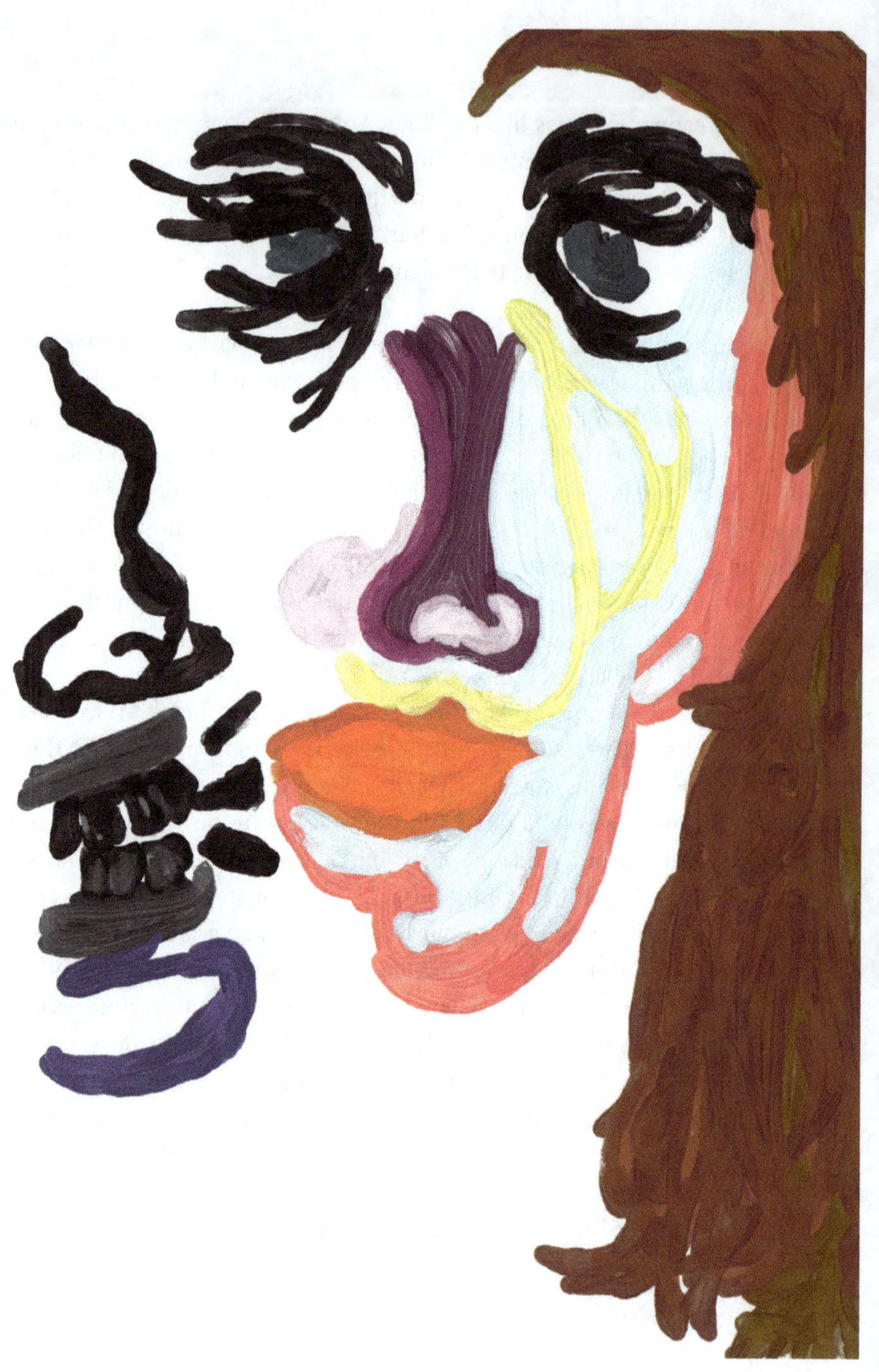

Trapped in Upstate New York During a Pandemic and Threatened by a Flesh-Clad Demon, the Fox-Haired Seer Sharpens the Edges of Her Skin and Meditates Upon the Parable of the Snowglobe

I witched the seasons and made it snow on his birthday that first
year that everyone hid in our homes from the poisonous air. I knew
how he loved winter weather, even in May, and I hoped the ice
beneath his tires would crystallize with the blow
and whiskey in his blood to guide him alone like a rogue, sublunary
parade float into the forever-after of a thick, unyielding oak. For how long
                                                            had he covered my world in snow?

                                    After he   me and then blamed me

for angering him into ugliness, my body transformed
into an opalescent glass globe. Inside the globe are
two tiny figurines, a man and a woman. They are
enjoying an indoor picnic of charcuterie that the man
has prepared in order to romance the woman,
so that she will not leave.   Richard Ramirez's
winged ghost holds the globe in the palm of his
hand sometimes, idly, as he sits in the midst of a
crackling fire. He eyes the figurines and I don't
know what he's thinking, or if he's thinking
anything at all. Every time I try to write you a letter
about the things that happened to me at the hands
of the man I loved and trusted, Richard Ramirez ruffles his beautiful, six-foot
-by-six-foot wings and smiles a terrifying smile, gives the incandescent
glass ball in his hand a good shake. I had wings like that
once, but more beautiful. My red-bearded man sheared them, sawed

through bone and sinew. Left me corrugated scars & daguerreotype
memory of *me*. The tiny woman inside the snow
globe begins to stand up. The man smashes
his fist down over her hand, which is pressed
against the table for support as she tries
to propel herself into exit. Richard Ramirez shakes
the opalescent glass ball and laughs because it's
fun to shake a snow globe, and glittering flakes fill
the entire thing until you almost can't see the
people inside. Each flake is a tiny jagged bit of
pearlescent metal, a razor sharper than anything
you've known. The snow fills the globe and the woman
keeps trying to stand and the man keeps
smashing the hand she used to write with.

Letter to Diane Arbus

Hooked, quick,
dactylic—he

thought he'd found his sweet pink
mitten of eternity in me

who could not sane
herself a stationary

sheet set. Me, I need to keep

It's the sweetest

among us whose hides become

acquainted with impressions
of heels; we acquiesce to taking

our quiet where
we can find it: razor blade learning

to unlink the cuffs of the skin

plummeting. As in

parachute wind.

Sisyphean.

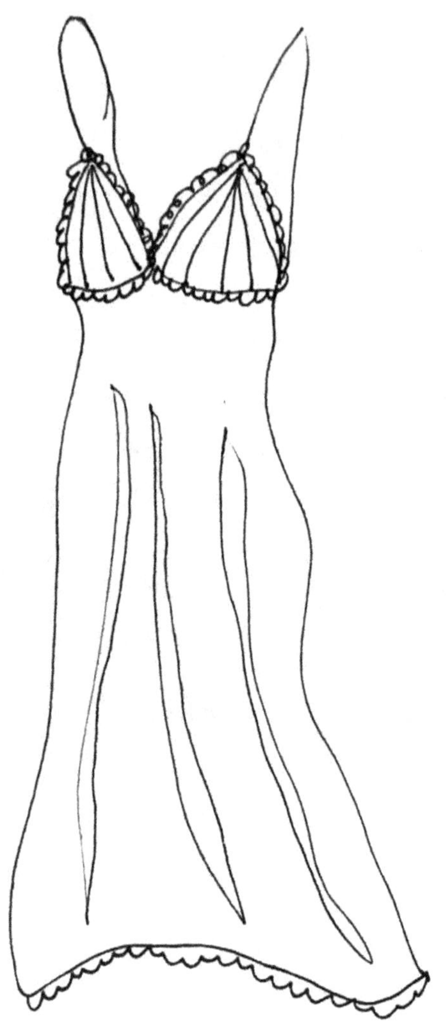

Exodus in X Minor

three months dreamless sleep like a battering

ram   pulverized

me
nightly to piceous watery piscina

until All Hallows Eve

my sublunary pilgrimage
to kiss iron
kiss the earth
heap silver to a hill, whip
the air with certain gestures
stack what copper tower
ask permission   & slip

darkly to the proper cross
look skyward, plead   & exit

withdraw, still facing forwards
shape exhale & exhortations
so no attachments may persist.   Upon arriving

home, a special bath   of pearl & grit.

Journey into dreamworlds. Wander
listen find

the terminal hotel see him
laughing, doing lines.
I expelled luminescent

pearls from my heart valves to his feet
his hands closed around my
throat my chest seizing to breathe

Spirits gathered like locusts I unfurled
my wings and screamed bled
from my mouth tawny burnished

castle into being all around us. My red

me to his chest *You have to leave*

now, he said. *Before it really is too late.* Forced me back
across the threshold I
awakened gasping throat stayed tender bruises raw for days

Erzsébet Báthory Returns the Fox-Haired Seer to Her Raven Roots and Commands Her to Drink the Blood of the Man Who Grabbed Her Violently and Said Into Her Face, If You Fuck With Any of My Money, I'll Kill You, Filthy Whore

Be no longer   girl   bound   soft bereft   self-guillotine

Release your worship like a murder

of ink-dark birds screaming   flight towards a man who has

set foot in a field they own.   Has stormed

your wrought iron fence love   has squeezed you nearly

gone   to fresh-dug grave

release your auburn   fox darting   through foliage

pursued by hounds & men   with guns   & knives for skinning   trail

your fingers   beneath mine   I will hold   you   I will

enlighten   endarken   imbue

you   wear your power like sound   avian   omen

oracle   striking   symphonies of fear into men   hear

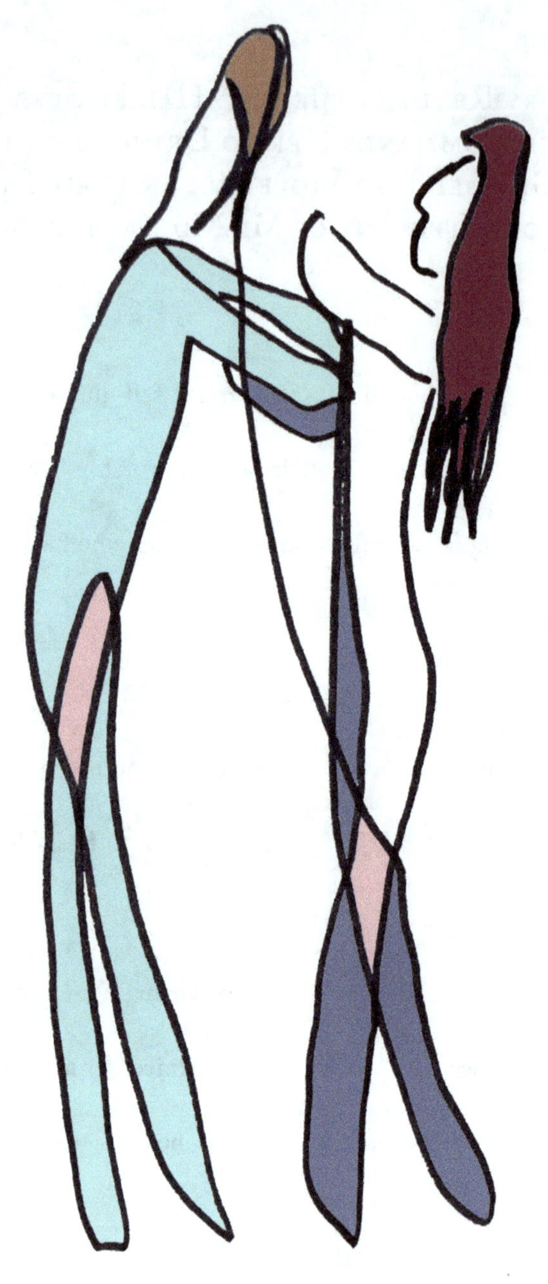

now   your sisters   gather under the raven   crown of night

light fires   hiss forbidden   language through his body

curse his veins   press   arrows to bow   brandish & thrust   sword blades

singing your name   You should have   been the one to cut his

throat   sever head from chest forever

see now the canal, bright

pink convulsing sinew   bubble purple   blood sacrifice

for your freedom.   Don't plead.   Place   your mouth to his

vile body one last time

open

yourself   throat of a bright starling

singing   make him prey

Letter to Diane Arbus

Less a howl, now,
at the moon than a hat
 brim over the eyes: orange

cylinder spilling pills like sun
flower seeds into your palm. The flash lost

                                        in a series of flashes.

                    (yes you wanted this
                    like tattoos)   Lonely as a dial tone.

Clare Was One of Four Catholic Workers in Ithaca, New York, Who Spilled Her Blood at a Military Recruitment Center to Protest the USA's Invasion of Iraq, and Was Subsequently Arrested and Imprisoned

Even nascent bodies
crave pleasance. Dreams
delivered by celestial

fire fall fallow. Soft belly,
not without grace Crawling,
we learn to rise where to place

the self like a chalice in brume
steel-bound wrists whirling lights like ice
floes before dawn Immersed: our ceremonial

nerves in quieted hours find
calm in ascetic cells
cathedrals arctic solace aurora Polaris

like skyflower jessamine we climb
clinging yet to ground Through
heather though esker solaris

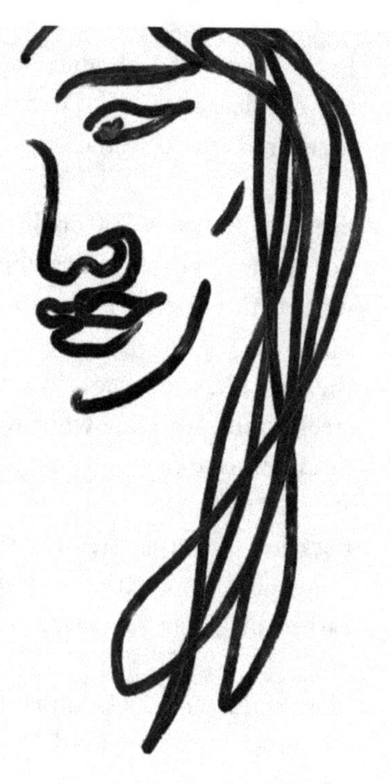

The Raven-Haired Seer Selects a Card from Her Own Handmade Oracle Deck to Symbolize The Querent On Her True Path, and the Image Is the Woman King of Bones and Stars

Vortex-hexed, dark-wooded glen.   Trailing drops

of her blood : desperate compass.   Crepuscular, winged, septenary-

headed   viper   bared carnassial teeth   came clawing.   Bright scars

on her skin   tales buried in flesh   pulsed light through her breathless

body   resplendent   dimmed kingdom

relentless   cimmerian eyes shone

& froze   her heart   holding each heavier   incomplete heave

unable to close   exploded

trees dropped swollen blossoms   panic-petaled grace

stars spilling fiery through tangled boughs   around her moonlit face

She rises again like origin   (tenebrous   flamelike)

mane   swirling windswept from crown:

aurora   floods   nebulous sky   orisons for her

psyche like Pangea   pulling

light & water down

from ash   her bones shine   through   like vixen

eyes in the night.   Know there will never be another

place she cannot see you: She will change your life.

The Raven-Haired Seer Crowns Herself King

sloe baptism
scented balsam

breathe in   fountain erupting from ground
fire falling from sky   meteoric   howling

unfasten yourself now

obsidian-washed   plume-dazzled

dampen myrrhic balm
of Gilead

anoint yourself embrocate each tress
consecrate your head

close your lids
mirror-cool   & feel

yourself move sands upon what
Persephonian shore   dark river   reverent, swirls

admits her   sacred person   each season
she returns, Stygian sovereign

waters lap to kiss her soles & then recede retreat
But flow supine & reaching plead to caress her hem once more

Navigate these violet rapids
as Mór Ríoghan

attends the deaths of kings
wingspan fearless above battlefield

& dark-throated sings
each plume a holy tongue against the wind

Let the silken, satin-certain
bloodfall drench your silver-curtain psyche

as you pull it open fast & cup
your palms unsealing ravenous your core

feed your unflinching revelling revealing
know: you'll bleed & always keen but never again pour

yourself into another's chalice, beauty
splashed against a callous

maladjusted ballast,
rapacious millstone

man who thinks his phallus is a scepter
& you new ocean to explore

Feel tufted weight upon your skull: raven
diadem starred black pearls & hematite

each jet quill a baubled onyx blossom
spangled   peacock ore

bejeweling spiked wrought-iron   like foliage
undulating down   from boughs   of sacred sycamore

tiara of jet-diamond   terror   & power   won with
blood   set   flowing   lapidarian   to adorn   your sovereign

body   witch   you
shall be taken   shall be stolen   felled or cloven

never more.

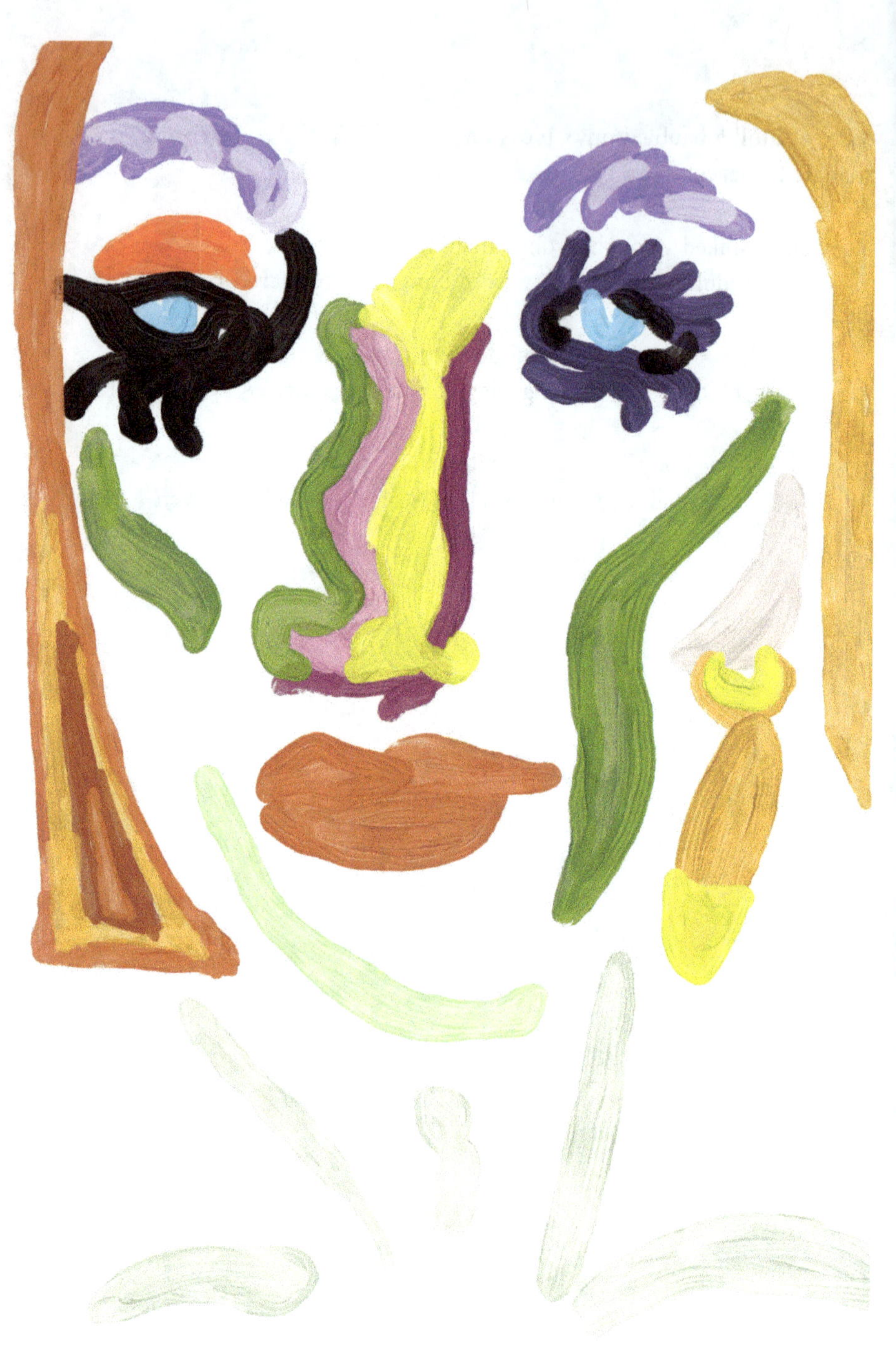

The Sunny-Haired Undertaker's Daughter and the Raven-Haired Cartographers' Daughter Write Letters Amidst the Pandemic

We were neighbors for years in Manhattan and never knew it. We moved back
into our childhood homes in our twilight town, during the years of contagion.

The cemetery between us a sanctuary; hills turning bright,
chill spreading. We mull wine and send photographs: orange

zest, a splash of juice, cinnamon sticks, cloves, small-bubble
simmered in burgundy. We make soup with garlic and fennel.

My hyssop is nearly gone, I tell Matilda. The purples were wild
this summer. I rescued a hound from the floorless

basement he was left to starve in. I named him Cúchulainn,
the king's own protector. I am king of my body, as Mélusine,

mermaid who refused to cede the secrets of her body to a man.
I own and wear my raven crown, protected by tooth and claw. I send

photographs of Cúchulainn; Matilda reveals images of herself in other
epochs—haunted, lavish, each surface draped and illuminated in twilight.

I send her photos of Évangéline and Grey, trotting around the equestrian
ring, their shared blur of motion like celestial fog. Matilda and I talk

about grief. About how to make up the dead,
style their hair and clothing. Could we guide

the bereft as her father did? Map unknown terrain like my parents,
reopen the mysterious halls of our youth? Her father passed on

some years ago. *I think about us doing this almost every day,* she says.
I move my basil and rosemary indoors before the first killing

frost. I have four kinds of mint, some wild
bergamot. She tells me of a woman who found a dark-

hearted man and helped him hurt other women: this woman
now fixates on her. I sew the sunny-haired undertaker's daughter

a pandemic mask with nazar boncuğu on it. Nazar, Nazarene, as in
Marys visiting the dead together, two women pulling back

boulders, facing death to care for the body of a loved one,
calmly gazing into truth and ghosts while men hid—

weeping, fearful. We come from women who don't fear pain
the way men fear pain. Women who taught their daughters

to be one another's shepherds, sisters; to heal the sick, to sew
clothing. To make soup and tea, medicinal tinctures, conjure

courage where none yet exists. Matilda and I are
our mothers' daughters. We protect each other.

Exodus in X Minor

I've been gifted an earth
of foxes by the Mother: they've nested

on my land. I catch them,
flashes of bright auburn moving

fluidly through the late spring
snow, then vanishing. I savor

bitter coffee, notes of cocoa. Somewhere
inside my body, I am still

in Assateague, watching wild horses on the shore.
Somewhere, I never left the Coney Island sea.

I set my phonograph
needle down. I've been up all night, talking,

talking about folklore, prayer, the soul of a friend
who recently met with the change called death. I've had

love again, since the end of my
gouging, red-bearded

travesty. I forgave myself. My next lover, a chemist, loved me
madly, because he was mad. I keep myself

company, these days. I enjoy myself
& wait & wait & wait for my true partner

my sweetest friend to find me. I have
no idea how I'll know them, no

idea whether they are truly traveling
furiously towards me at unimaginable speed.

I've been keeping my blood
at a steady thrum been keeping myself masked, locked

away (like everyone, these months,
air alchemized toxic

in our lungs), separate. I learned to run
again, the gross alchemy of sweat, hard

breath punching in the chest. I fell on ice, down
a paved hill, tore my knee apart, sprained my ankle.

I healed myself:
Scarred, proud.

The morning glories and moonflowers are hail-battered
but climbing already, magenta-splattered and royal

purple mixing with oceanic blue, immaculate night-pure
whites staying open through morning fog. I'll have sunflowers by July,

pink Scotch heather in December. My daughter picks strawberries
from our land. *Ours are sweetest, Mommy.* Évangéline's favorite

book is *The Night Gardener*, about people learning to create beauty from the earth, and beauty

creating love within them. I built myself
new altars, on this land. Jewel-toned, rich.

I built myself a gilded bed,
ensconced in soft blue cloud.

We drove for days to sit on the rocky shores of Lake Superior with Brigid
and her daughter Luna in bracing wind. Évangéline cast stones to the waters,

her first best-friend Luna collecting the most beautiful and strange
they could find, presenting them to us as gifts, mementos of our time.

Évangéline rubs the pink ocean-tumbled quartz of rose and shadow
as she relaxes into sleep. The glittering sandstone rests, asparkle

on one of my altars, alongside the raven feathers Brigid sent.
I marvelled at her crocuses—the way they spread across her yard,

invincible. Another gift from the Mother:
I remember my dreams again, wake knowing

I am everything
that I still carry.

I own all that I have
chosen to lay down.

I Live in the Shadow Hills

When I was eight years old, I first visited the violent place where I would make my adult home: where I would first read Joan Didion, where I would experience wildfires and earthquakes firsthand, where I would come to understand the Manson murders as a point of cultural fixation. Where I would marry my high school sweetheart (in Rancho Palos Verdes, where Joan Didion once lived). Where I would try to look evil squarely in the face and figure out what to do next.

I travelled to the Los Angeles area many times as a child. We had family in Orange County, and winter visits to their homes provided relief from the ice and isolation of upstate New York. From a young age, I have been mesmerized by the wildfires and earthquakes that television news stations brought into my family's living room. That people I loved, and to whom I was related, were in proximity to these cataclysmic events of the natural world made the events real to me in a way that they otherwise likely would not have been.

The year I was eight, the city burned for several days as riots spread in reaction to the verdict that allowed police to walk free after the videotaped beating of Rodney King. The National Guard was stationed around the University of Southern California; 17 years after the riots, and 18 years after the beating itself, I would begin my performance there as a doctoral candidate.

When I finally moved to Los Angeles from New York in my early twenties, I stayed with a family in Laguna Hills named the Palmers. My then-partner, Iago, and I had been invited to stay with them for six months; we stayed for about six weeks. One day early in our stay, I noticed a house in the Palmers' expansive neighborhood with a lot of birds on the roof and in the yard. There was netting around the house that I thought was intended to keep the birds in. I wondered if they were exotic pets, or if the homeowners might be avian breeders or dealers. Molly explained to me that, rather, the nets were intended to help keep the birds out. She told me that about twenty years earlier, her eldest daughter had befriended the newly adopted daughter of the couple who owned the Bird House. The girl was an orphan from a European country that Molly did not name. Molly said that she had thought the young girl a little odd; she had a preoccupation with cats. More than that, really, Molly elaborated, the girl seemed to have a minor obsession with trying to seem catlike—a tendency presented in the manner of an idée fixe. Molly had thought that it might be a byproduct of the young girl's rough life before being adopted into an affluent Southern Californian family. The little girl had likely not had much in the way of socialization or even formal education. Perhaps she had had a feline friend at the orphanage. Or had wished for one.

One night, Molly told me, she and Ken went out and left their daughter in the care of a babysitter; they had allowed their daughter to invite her new friend to their house for a sleepover. They had only been gone for a short time when the babysitter called them, frantic. The little girl obsessed with cats had wedged herself under Molly and Ken's bed. Underneath her jacket she was covered in blood that did not appear to be her own. The little cat girl had killed her adoptive parents' cats before coming to attend the sleepover. She said that she had drunk their blood before deciding to wear some of it, "for strength." She claimed that her adoptive family wanted to kill her, and this was a mode of self-protection—a means of gathering strength. After she was sent away to a psychiatric facility, birds began to flock to the house, congregating everywhere.

I found the story difficult to believe. Despite my skepticism, I avoided passing the Bird House, taking extra turns and driving down extra streets. I did not want to be near the place. I could not say exactly why I didn't want to be near it, but my propensity for avoidance seemed a harmless self-indulgence—a quirk. After we moved out of the neighborhood, however, I continued to think about the little girl, about the house, and about the shadow of birds that seemed to constantly hover over it. I had never regarded the appearance of animals as ominous before moving to Southern California.

***

When I was eleven, I wrote a short story about attempting to confront evil directly, and I happened to name the protagonist, a stand-in for myself, Winnifred Chapman. Both names had (unrelated) personal significance to me.

When I was twenty-nine, I began an essay about the Manson murders. It was then that I learned the identity of the real Winnifred Chapman[1]. I admitted Iago's cruelty to myself, and left. I began dating my high school sweetheart, Cas—whose real name is Casimir, a nod to the French part of his ancestry. Casimir vaguely hates France, although he has never been to France and cannot articulate the reason for his disdain. Nevertheless, he insists—and has insisted, since we were both fourteen years old—on being called Cas. Cas and I had shared an affinity for *The Downward Spiral* upon its initial release. For Cas, I moved back to upstate New York, a place that had been the setting for grisly murders of several young women when I was growing up. And, during the year that I was twenty-nine, Cas would introduce me to two different men who would both soon, in unrelated circumstances, murder their wives.

If you add eight, eleven, and twenty-nine together, their sum equals forty-eight. And it had, as I finished the first draft of this piece in August of 2017, been forty-eight years since the Manson murders took place.

Of course, as soon as I noticed this, I was certain that it meant nothing. And yet since I have noticed this pattern of numeric connection, it retains my focus even after I have placed my focus elsewhere. It nags at me. I am not sure why, or what I am supposed to do with it.

I struggled, during the year that I was twenty-nine, and for many years after, with admitting Cas's cruel streak. Sometimes I ignored it because I thought he would protect me from a world that is often cruel, dangerous, and hostile specifically towards women. Sometimes, when he turned his cruel streak on me, I rationalized that it wasn't really coming from him, that this tendency in him had evolved as a survival mechanism due to the circumstances in which he grew up. I pushed it out of my mind, even when he was arrested for assault six months after we started

[1] Winnifred Chapman was Polanski and Tate's housekeeper. She found the victims' bodies at 10050 Cielo Drive, the morning after the murders took place, and telephoned the police.

dating. Even a few months after that, when I saw him assault a fast-food employee and evade arrest because the employee declined to press charges.

Name redacted WHO IS AN EMPLOYEE OF THIS LOCATION CALLED TO REPORT A CUSTOMER THREW A DRINK AT HIM. redacted STATED THE MALE OPERATOR OF A DARK COLORED car make & model redacted NO redacted DOORS redacted THREW redacted AT HIM THRU THE DRIVE

redacted THE PLATE # redacted WAS TAKEN BY THE ASST. MANAGER. THE VEHICLE CAME BACK SUSPENDED TO redacted redacted DECLINED TO GIVE A DEPOSITION OR TO PURSUE CHARGES AGAINST THIS MALE BUT I HAD redacted MAKE precinct redacted AWARE OF THE SUSPENDED VEHICLE INFO. NO FURTHER ACTION WAS TAKEN AT THIS TIME.

***

During my brief and turbulent stay at the Palmer residence, Molly requested my help with moving a kitchsy-looking statue from its perch at one end of their outdoor pool to the other, near the lagoon-style hot tub. Molly asked for my help because, she said, she could tell I was a witch. She, who had been raised traditional Southern Christian, asked me to raise up some energies so that we could move this statue, which must have weighed at least a couple hundred pounds. She said she had seen some nuns do this raising of energies once—nothing Satanic or occult about it—and one of the nuns, well, she was a nun but she was also a witch. Mildly flattered by this odd idea regarding my magical capacities to displace formidable physical obstacles, I channeled my early adolescent experiences of "light as a feather, stiff as a board," and did my best to raise some energy. I felt foolish and a bit embarrassed. The statue wouldn't budge. The next morning, when we awoke, the statue had indeed been moved to the far end of the poolside. I asked Molly about it, awkwardly apologizing for my inability to help the way she had asked. She looked at me, puzzled. "But you did move it, Fox," she said. "I watched you move it." I was confused and embarrassed and uncomfortable. I said nothing else.

Molly chatted to us at dinner that night about crystals and crystal healings. Iago and I shared a conspiratorial glance. What kind of West Coast nonsense was this? A black widow spider repeatedly climbed the arch of Iago's foot under the table during the course of the meal. It did not bite him, but neither could he apprehend it. Every time I sighted it and he pulled back, it ran inside a crevice under the table. Molly told us not to worry. She said the world is full of these things, that they cannot be avoided. She herself had once been bitten.

The fires began in earnest that week. Iago had already hit me once, and had coerced sex from me multiple times. He had not yet begun ending minor arguments about housework by standing over me with a raised fist. *You know,* Molly once said to me in an exasperated tone, *you don't have to answer to him.* I had not yet come to the point of acknowledging Iago's cruelty and leaving him. But, in retrospect, I don't know why I wasn't more afraid of him by that time, or of what might have come next. It seemed, in my mind, somehow linked to the way I felt about the fires. They were objectively terrifying, but I had trouble feeling my fear; because of that, I had trouble understanding that I was afraid. I could not bring myself to believe that something like that might be the end of me.

***

Joan Didion is not the only writer to have made the connection that she so famously made between the Santa Ana winds and disturbances in human behavior, similar to those associated with the full moon. Raymond Chandler once described Los Angeles during a Santa Ana: "On nights like that, every booze party ends in a knife fight. Meek little wives feel the edge of the carving knife and study their husbands' necks. Anything can happen."[2] Didion relates, in a tone less dramatic, supportive reportage:

> ...doctors hear about headaches and nausea and allergies, about 'nervousness,' about 'depression.' In Los Angeles, some teachers do not attempt to conduct formal classes during a Santa Ana, because the children become unmanageable.

Though her extended description of the Santa Ana and its effects sounds almost like magical realism, Didion's reportage is accurate. Positive ions and negative ions tend to have opposing effects on us. Studies have indicated that negative ions possess anti-microbial properties[3], and exert mood-stabilizing effects[4] on

[2] Chandler, Raymond. "Red Wind." 1938.
[3] https://www.ncbi.nlm.nih.gov/pmc/articles/PMC2873555/
[4] https://www.webmd.com/balance/features/negative-ions-create-positive-vibes#1

human beings by augmenting serotonin levels.[5] Negative ions, naturally generated when water molecules collide, explain why many people find showers refreshing, and oceanside stays rejuvenating. Positive ions, naturally generated by *föhn* winds like the Santa Ana, tend to cause humans tension, aggression, and general malaise.

It troubles me that so many of us reflexively mistrust the connections between the earth and our bodies—that we often need these things "proven" before we accept their reality. Our bodies, after all, are recycled celestial matter; we are literally, as Joni Mitchell sang, stardust.[6] [7] Because we know that we are of this planet, it's hard to understand our relationship with it sometimes—the way we terrorize and damage it, the way we have so little faith in our deep and ancient connection to it. The way we are surprised when our Earth sometimes violently cleanses herself of our abusive presence—through virus, through wind and fire, through the violent tendencies coded into human DNA that often motivate us to obliterate one another in pursuit of resources. As Didion explains:

> Los Angeles weather is the weather of catastrophe, of apocalypse, and, just as the reliably long and bitter winters of New England determine the way life is lived there, so the violence and the unpredictability of the Santa Ana affect the entire quality of life in Los Angeles, accentuate its impermanence, its unreliability. The wind shows us how close to the edge we are.

Didion was correct, I think, that people who have not lived in Los Angeles have a difficult time understanding how radically the Santa Ana and its apocalyptic conjurings figure into local culture. Los Angeles has many ways of observing and remembering past traumas. We internalize via earthquake drills and the quietly anxious hypervigilance of fire season, but also through guided tours about celebrity murders, serial killers, violent historical events, grisly and tragic deaths of young and vulnerable people. They are, of course, colloquially known as "tourist traps."

[5] https://inspiredliving.com/surround-air-ionizers/negative-ions-serotonin.htm

[6] Worrall, Simon. "How 40,000 Tons of Cosmic Dust Falling to Earth Affects You and Me." *National Geographic*. January 28, 2015. https://www.nationalgeographic.com/news/2015/01/150128-big-bang-universe-supernova-astrophysics-health-space-ngbooktalk/#-close

[7] Schrivjer, Iris and Karel. *Living with the Stars: How the Human Body is Connected to the Life Cycles of the Earth, the Planets, and the Stars.* Oxford University Press, 2015.

You take the shiny bait, and get snapped up into—something. The unspeakable is spoken by a hype-man, over a loudspeaker, for your entertainment. The unthinkable becomes an attraction—becomes attractive. We have shrines to this violence, which we term museums. Amusement mausoleums. One such enterprise is the Museum of Death in Hollywood.

***

I thought that Cas, who proposed to me in Las Vegas and then twice in Los Angeles, was the love of my life. I grew up with the saying that once is an accident, twice is a coincidence, and three times is the truth. Cas asked me three times, I said yes three times, and then we got married three times. But I understood even then that Cas was a conduit for my connection to a very dark place—the hometown we share with Rod Serling, in upstate New York, that I believe to be a spiritual vortex. When I moved back for a year to be with Cas, he introduced me to two different men who would both soon become murderers. Despite the intense and enduring love I felt for Cas—which a doctor would later explain to me as a traumatic bond, and not real love at all—I have only contempt and revulsion for the types of violence he has chosen to embrace, and the dark ways in which those violences have shaped him.

And yet, I also understand the place from which Cas comes in more academic terms. It is brutal—the sort of which cosmopolitan and affluent suburban Americans would prefer to pretend does not exist. Cas's hard-drinking, thrill-seeking, drug-addled, blue-collar subculture of a dying industrial town is nestled among the intersections of various dearths of opportunity. Because the degrees of difference separating punishment from reward exist on such a minute scale, in this place, there are really only a few types of social currency that one can hope to possess. One of those few significant currencies is a sense of dominance, almost always expressed in terms of physicality. Which almost always means violence or the threat of violence.

Narrative:
Complainant's name redacted states that name redacted a bouncer at location name redacted bar head botted him in the face. name redacted are

In the culture of the place I am describing, the physical dominance expressed by a man in public settings will be granted socially, by extension, to his female partner (if he has one) for as long as they are romantically linked. It is a sort of power garnered by association. One of the effects of this complicated social contract is that male aggression tends to be appreciated and actively encouraged by female romantic partners, even if they understand that same aggression as personally destructive to them. The credibility of one's physical dominance and power are absolutely central to the quality of life one may carve out for oneself. As far as I have been able to gather through immersion and observation, in order to maintain this type of credibility in such an environment, you must assume that everyone around you is willing to physically hurt you—and that they may even want to. For a man like Cas, who is used to overpowering any opponent in a physical altercation, this expectation is not the same thing as fear: it is worn like a badge, with a certain amount of swagger. He would like you to make him prove how tough he is.

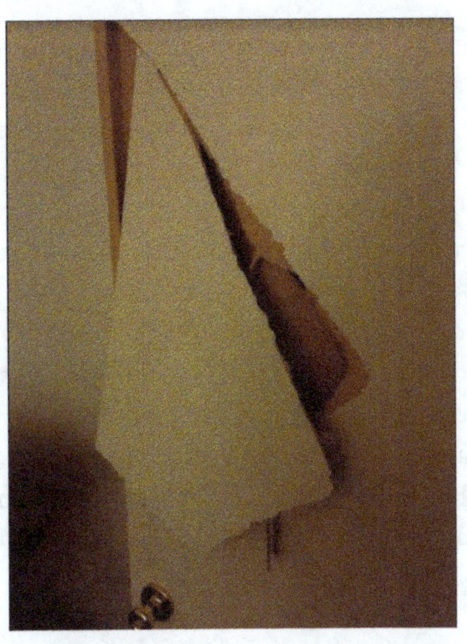

I tried to talk to Cas about this once; his reaction was to lash out. I interpreted his aggression as hurt feelings, and never brought up the topic again. But, as Audre Lorde observed so many decades ago, "My silences had not protected me. Your silence will not protect you." This proved literally true: one morning, a little over a year into our marriage, Cas asked me why I was being so quiet. Surprised, I reassured him several times that nothing was wrong, that I was simply drinking coffee and hanging out with him in our living room on an early weekend morning, and didn't have much to say. Cas, who had already consumed several shots of bourbon, began to scream at me that I was weaponizing my silence in order to punish him for some imagined offense. After several attempts to reiterate that nothing was wrong, and that I was not upset with him, I got up and went into the bedroom. I heard Cas get up to follow me into the bedroom. I was scared; I locked the door. Cas punched through the door. Terrified, I tried to leave. Cas blocked the path to our apartment door with his body and asked me in a very quiet voice not to go. He said that the door shouldn't have caved under his fist like that, that it was poorly made. That I shouldn't have locked the door, because he had the right to go into any room of his house that he wanted. Terrified, I agreed to stay.

***

Cas drove us to the Death Museum in my Volkswagen Beetle, the car that I chose and bought for myself after I left Iago. Cas and I were hit twice on the freeway that year, both times in my little white car. Both times, the other drivers were at fault.

When we first came to Los Angeles together, Cas drove a Wrangler: doorless, topless. We drove this way on the freeways. After two weeks, I said to him calmly, matter-of-factly, *You know, if someone were to hit us on the freeway with the car in this state, I would probably die. I don't mean that I would be injured or paralyzed: I mean that I would probably actually die.* He looked at me, surprised; then he went outside and put the doors and top on the car, and didn't say another word about it. I wondered then, and again as we drove to the Museum of Death, what it must be like to move through the world without a persistent, tenacious consciousness of all the things present, at any given moment, that can kill you.

***

Cas and I secretly eloped in Vegas before our real wedding with friends and family. We went to Vegas a lot, in those days. We usually didn't plan in advance. One of us would say to the other in Friday traffic, "Wanna hit up Vegas instead of going home?" and the other would respond, usually, along the lines of, "Challenge accepted." It was a short drive through the desert, which I believed to have purifying properties. It was a nice portal into and out of Sin City, which we liked less for the sin and more for the larger-than-life ridiculousness. We used to joke that the only real difference between Las Vegas and Los Angeles is that people who live in Las Vegas are in on the joke. There's some truth to that, but I no longer think it is the only real difference.

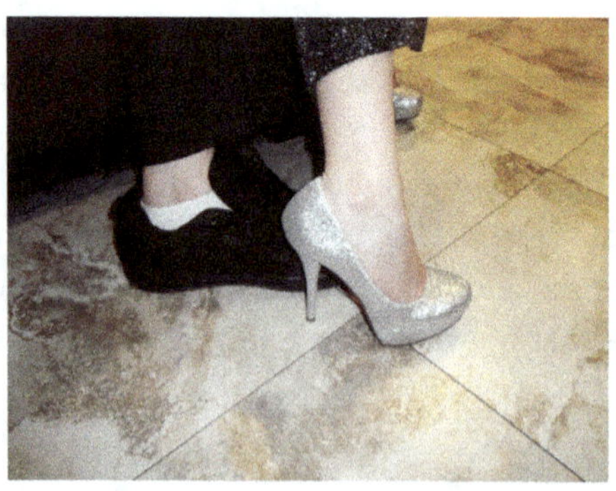

Forty-eight years after the Manson murders, Cas and I settled into married life in a haunted town in the Shadow Hills of Los Angeles County. And forty-eight years after the Manson murders, a lone gunman stayed in a Vegas hotel quite familiar to us, near where we got married, and opened fire on thousands of people attending a concert.

***

Something that particularly struck me during our deeply unpleasant time at the Museum of Death in Hollywood was its confirmation of the Cielo Drive murders as some sort of cultural touchstone for many Americans. Why do we love to fixate on the fact that this one person who killed people—who masterminded the killing of people—liked the song "Helter Skelter"? What is behind our cultural focus on those several people who were killed by him, and by his Family, at this particular address? More to the point, it is not as though America has *not* perpetrated far grislier, and wider-scale, crimes against humanity than this incident. Why does it stand out in the way that it does? It is true that those murders were horrific. But all murders are horrific, and many around the globe are probably equally or more so—though the competitive comparison of horrific murders feels like a fool's errand.

I think that part of our macabre fascination with this particular crime, as embodied by its unholy shrine at the Death Museum in Hollywood, is that the people murdered at 10050 Cielo Drive were not only racially and socioeconomically very privileged, but some of them were famous. In popular American imagination, this would have been expected to somehow protect them from such acts of violence. To prevent them from experiencing ultimate helplessness. This crime keeps its place in our collective consciousness in part because people are fearful of the knowledge that these are false promises. If socioeconomic acumen and cultural power won't keep people safe from one another, then is it possible that nothing could?

I think that many people also enjoy knowing that these things are false promises, that even the wealthy and privileged—often people who exert oppressive influence in the lives of others—are not always as secure as they might seem. Tate's husband, Polanski, visibly ranked among them: in recent years women have come forward with narratives of assault perpetrated against them in their teenage years by Polanski. If predators are not entirely insulated from the viciousness of the outside world, then perhaps those of them who seem to evade justice might not do so forever.

The convergence of vague attraction, disgust, and discomfort that America seems to feel about the Cielo Drive murders is similar, and I think related, to our grotesque historical relationship with "conventionally pretty" female victimhood: there is an element of hating it, and an element of loving to hate it. And there is an element of simply loving it. How many Americans would celebrate Sharon Tate on the same level if she had instead taken out a gun and blown holes through the bodies of those who sought to harm her? Isn't part of her legacy and her mystique that the gentle, blonde Madonna figure simply pleaded, helplessly and selflessly—and fruitlessly—for the life of her unborn baby?

And, Manson was a cult leader. America loves a cult leader.

***

My parents had a friend, back in the 1960s, whose name was Charlie Manson. I didn't know about this until I was twenty-nine years old, living alone in Los Angeles and considering the infamy of the Manson murders that took place at 10050 Cielo Drive. Charlie Manson left Charles Manson's "Family" right before they began killing people. He wouldn't say why, although he did confide in my parents, and in his twin, that Charles Manson was "one scary cat." I know that they spent time in the desert together, using either mescaline or peyote to experience "visions." I don't know what the visions were of, and I don't know what the catalyst was for Charlie Manson deciding to leave the Family.

But it's not difficult to imagine that—for one utterly hypothetical example—in the 1960s, Jack Nicholson, Roman Polanski, and Warren Beatty might have trolled the Sunset Strip, looking for naive young women to pick up and sexually abuse. Drugs were highly accessible, and wealthy, famous, white men rarely, if ever, got into trouble regarding assault. It's not difficult to imagine they might at some point have picked up a girl who was either already associated with the Manson Family, or who might have later decided to join. Right? It's possible to picture Charles Manson, already an unstable person, becoming enraged, then obsessed with the idea of retaliation for an assault against one of "his" women. I am able to envision Charlie Manson finding the apparition of this incensed shadow-self to be unnerving, and getting out while the getting's still good. Perhaps Charles blamed Polanski and his dissolute associates for Charlie's desertion of the Family, as well. Perhaps Manson remained fixated on punishing Polanksi until the murders were been executed. His rage might have prevented him from sympathy for Polanksi and Tate's unborn son, his sense of justice so perverted that he was gratified to hear of Tate crying out for her mother as the knife tore her body. He might have told his Family, This is divine justice. We have done to Polanski what Polanski did to us. To our family.

***

Next we hear of Polanski, he's posing for *LIFE* next to his front door, where PIG is still visibly written in his late wife's blood.

Next we hear of him after that—everyone knows this story: the helpless thirteen-year-old girl at Jack Nicholson's house, who cries and protests despite the quaaludes and other drugs as Polanksi assaults her multiple times—tortures her. For a long time, people will react to this narrative as though the only thing wrong with it was that the girl was underage. As though there is an appropriate age for a woman to suffer acts of torture. We know that Angelica Huston, also present in the house at the time, hears the girl's screams and pleas, but does nothing to interfere with the assault or help the victim of Polanski's acts of torture. We are never told if Angelica Huston feels, or felt, helpless. Whoopi Goldberg tells us on an episode *The View*, "But it wasn't *rape*-rape." We are never told if she feels helpless, either.

Decades later, Roman Polanski makes a poignant film titled *The Pianist*, and it wins awards at important ceremonies and festivals he cannot attend for fear of arrest. Adrian Brody wins an Academy Award for his performance in the film. Halle Berry reads Adrian Brody's name out of the envelope. Brody runs up on stage, grabs her, forcibly bends her over backwards, and shoves his tongue into her mouth in front of everyone. In the moments after the assault, still onstage, Halle Berry uses her fingers to clean his saliva from her face. "I bet they didn't tell you that was in the gift bag," Brody says at the microphone, and the audience laughs.

The next day, entertainment news reporters describe the kiss as a fun/ny stunt, and one notes that Halle Berry "good-naturedly played along." In all the coverage of the nonconsensual kiss, I did not see anyone use the word "assault." I was a teenager when this happened.

I expressed doubt, privately, to a friend of mine who was slightly older: Was I crazy? Was I overreacting? My friend seemed offended by my self-doubt. "He fucking *mauled* her," she responded, indignant, as though I should know better than to feel confused. I felt both shamed and reassured by her reaction—and still confused. If the answer was so clear, why I couldn't I seem to find it anywhere other than inside myself? For how long has our culture applauded while women are assaulted by men, often in front of other people, often while the assault is photographed or filmed—that is to say, while the assault is treated by witnesses as entertainment? And how long has our culture condoned or excused, in particular, the assault of Black women by white men? And if someone assaults you in front of a crowd, and not a single person appears to find it upsetting—if everyone treats it as entertainment—well, then what? That's always been the implication, hasn't it—*What are you doing to do about it?*

***

Molly had told Iago and me about being bitten by a black widow spider as a small child: *I was healthy enough that I got sick right away*, she said, which I didn't understand at the time. You could say that, in this particular instance, I was healthy enough to get sick right away.

We were not, as a culture, healthy enough for this poison to make us sick right away.

***

Trent Reznor recorded *The Downward Spiral* in the living room of 10050 Cielo Drive. Cas and I listened to that album together in high school; it was one of the few areas in which our musical tastes overlapped. Reznor set up the necessary equipment, some furniture, and named the house Le Pig Studios.

On one hand, I find this behavior sensationalist, exploitative, and disgusting. On the other hand, I think I understand some of the impulse behind it. To place oneself in an erstwhile torture chamber is to expose oneself to the energy of those who suffered there—and of those who caused the suffering. There is an element of vulnerability to this sort of immersion; and to place oneself in danger is to force adaptation. To hurt oneself is to evoke feeling. And, as E. E. Cummings tells us, feeling is first. As in, *I hurt myself today/ to see if I still feel.*

If we force ourselves to be vulnerable in this way—to respond to horror without the luxury of artifice or boundaries—perhaps we might defeat helplessness by first embracing it. Out of this, the artist creates some sort of transformative response. Spiritually minded people create the transformative energies released through prayer or other ritual.

But even the purest version of this impulse often has ugly results. For example, among many academics and creative people, there exists an obscene and unquestioned myth that if we make art or construct dialogue—*participate in the discourse*—in response to evil in the world, we are somehow less helpless than those who do not react in these "creative" ways. Art, like prayer, is apparatus; it can be perverted into a self-indulgent illusion. Art and prayer have both been used frequently as excuses to avoid doing any more pedestrian types of work to better the world. To avoid walking through any areas of real risk or danger. To avoid consequences that might disabuse participants of the notion that they and they alone are writing this narrative.

And forty-eight years after the Manson murders, Harvey Weinstein was held publicly accountable for his abuse of young women. It had gone on for decades, and was public knowledge. But the Oscars crowd seemed, suddenly, less willing to pretend that assault is a funny stunt. Accusations against many powerful men in the entertainment industry followed. But even some men who called out this type of abuse were themselves abusers. Ben Affleck posted a statement berating Weinstein, only to have strangers share footage of him humiliating a young actress on live television by groping her breast. Ben Affleck tweeted, "I behaved inappropriately... and I sincerely apologize." Ben Affleck has the reputation of protecting his younger brother's career in Hollywood since the time that said younger brother was sued for sexually harassing and abusing multiple female co-workers.

During this strange time, I dreamed a lot. I had not yet received any medical evidence that the baby I was carrying would be a girl. But I had multiple dreams in which she was both a girl and a king—a force mighty and celestial. During that strange time, I would not have wanted that energy—those emotions, that stress, those chemicals—inflicted on any baby I might be carrying; however, to expose a girl to that while she was still being formed inside my body, her first protector—I couldn't. I couldn't. The hyperemesis gravidarum that I suffered during my pregnancy helped me, in a way: I would otherwise have felt specifically sick at the idea of pushing her outside of my body into a world made and terrorized by men.

Joan Didion appears to have feared that she was some sort of possessed conduit for evil. Some sort of vessel for the occult, someone whose body perpetrated some sort of violent connection to Tate, through Polanski and her nebulous proximity to him. She says, *writing has not helped me to see what it means*. I think this means, perhaps, that Didion both sees and fears what it could mean, and that fear stops her from articulating it, quite. Writing of a similar reaction for *Vanity Fair*, years later, Lili Anolik suggests that Joan Didion would not allow herself to mention the possibility of the occult in this context:

> Didion and the Manson murders were linked, if only in Didion's mind. She sees occult significance in the fact that Polanski, at a party he attended with Tate, had spilled red wine on the dress she wore to her wedding, and that she and he were godparents to the same child, even if she can't figure out exactly what that significance is, even if her cool intelligence won't allow her to use the word "occult." Yet there's no question of the guilt in her tone. Is that because

> she felt somehow responsible for him? Did she believe he was a hallucination she'd conjured mid-migraine (her "vascular headache[s] of blinding severity")? A vision sprung to life during her psychic collapse the summer before (from the doctor's report: "In [the patient's] view she lives in a world of people moved by strange, conflicted, poorly comprehended, and, above all, devious motivations")? Her bad juju ("I remember a babysitter telling me that she saw death in my aura") made flesh?[8]

Forty-eight years after the Manson murders, Charles Manson died. He died twelve days after the airing of the *AHS*: *Cult* episode that reenacted the 10050 Cielo Drive murders, a week after his birthday, and four days after I found out via prenatal test results that my dreams and intuitions had been accurate, that my baby is a girl. She was due in May of 2018; nine years earlier, Barkers Ranch had burned to the ground. The earth had begun trying to purify that part of itself—the part where Manson and his Family had dwelled. I moved to Los Angeles three months after the Barkers Ranch fire. On the morning of Manson's death, the New York Post ran the story, with the headline, "Charles Manson Is Rotting in Hell." Another paper, more local to me, ran the headline, "Charles Manson Dies in Bakersfield Hospital." I sometimes stop in Bakersfield on my way to Vegas. Cas and I stopped there on our way to get married.

***

Two weeks later, on my mother's birthday, Cas and I awoke at 3 a.m. to 50 mph winds shaking our windows. We read that Ventura was burning in the Thomas fire; as we left the house to get coffee before work, we could see that Angeles National Forest, just over the hill from us, was burning. It was not yet dawn, but despite the darkened sky, we could see bright red smoke rising over the mountainside. I realized, from Google Maps being shared by local news sources, that we were in the mandatory evacuation zone for what would eventually be named the Creek Fire.

[8] Anolik, Lili. "How Joan Didion the Writer Became Joan Didion the Legend," *Vanity Fair*, February 2016.

We left moments before the LAPD roped off our street to begin evacuating people. Due to the severity of my hyperemesis (I had at that point lost more than 10% of my body weight), we went to a hotel rather than the shelter. That night, the Rye Fire broke out. By the following evening, the Skirball Fire was devouring Bel-Air, near the Getty Museum. Celebrities, many of whom live in the area or are friendly with people who live in the area, were reacting on social media as though they had never heard of any of the other fires attacking the Los Angeles area. They were, however, genuine in their devastated reactions to the Skirball Fire. This is, I think, the way humans behave when we have spent a long time thinking, with increasing certainty, that wherever the fires are in the world, they are not in our house, and will not come to our house. Then, suddenly, our homes are on fire, and we are devastated.

The Creek Fire also burned thirty horses alive. I thought about those horses for weeks. What their final moments must have been like. I was silently obsessed with these memories, though they were not my own. You could say I was haunted. The Shadow Hills are haunted, and I live in the Shadow Hills.

***

On that first night of our evacuation, I dreamed that Cas and I were seeking refuge in a hotel from a Los Angeles wildfire. In the dream, our hotel room looked like our hotel room. I lay on the bed and prayed, asking God: Of what is the earth trying to cleanse itself with this fire? What purification, what form of absolution, are we halting when we artificially extinguish these flames, instead of letting them run their course and burn out as they intend? Cas evaporated from the dream. I sat up, alone, and looked into the mirror: I saw, as it rippled and blurred, that Charles Manson wanted to communicate with me. The hotel room began to swim around me. I felt that someone was coming at me—coming for me. I felt myself begin to lose control, to lose consciousness within the dream. *You are someone else/ I am still right here.*

"Manson?" I asked—an expression of familiarity that continues to disturb me even now. "Is that you?"

And all the voice said was **NO**. It was not the kind of "no" one utters to answer a yes-or-no question; it is the type of **NO** an authority figure hands down in order to deny permission absolutely—the kind that cannot be surpassed or negotiated against. I don't think it was Charles Manson's voice; it was both silent and too loud for the sound barrier. As that **NO** reverberated through my dream, and through my body, I awakened with a gasp. Cas was asleep next to me in the darkened room, our snoring dogs snuggled around my pregnant body. I grasped the white-gold crucifix necklace that Cas had given me the year before Christmas, then groped for the rosary that I had worn to bed—a treasured possession given to me when I was five years old. As I felt for it, I realized that it was now broken in two places, and that pieces of the bottom part, containing the crucifix, prayers to the collective Trinity, and earliest Hail Marys, were scattered under me on the bed.

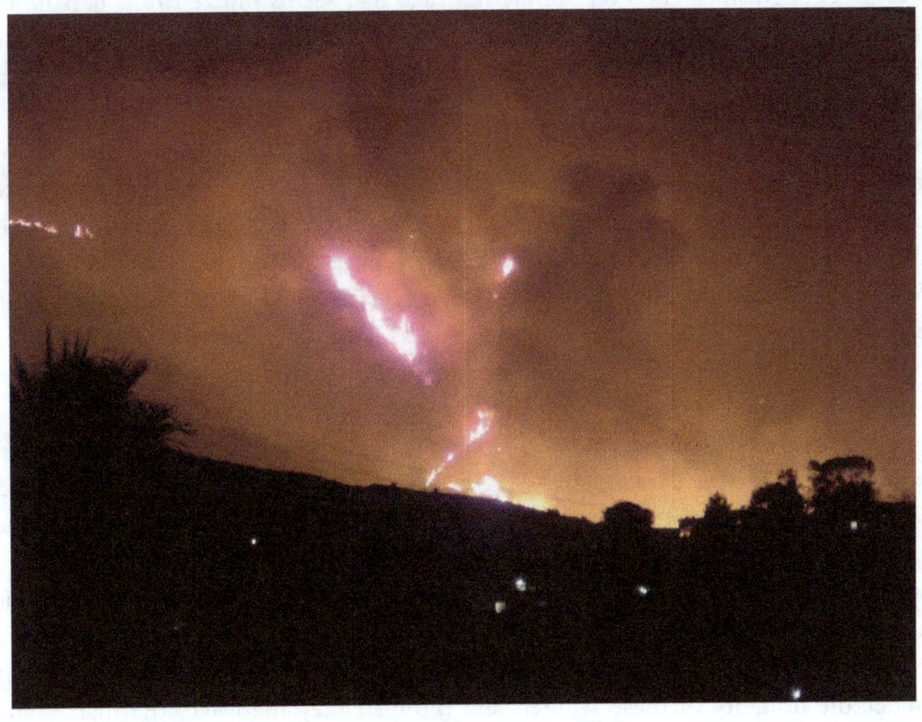

***

Several times during our marriage, Cas pointed out that when I was in certain states of mind—usually focused ones—the lights in whatever room we occupied would turn themselves on and off, repeatedly. Sometimes this happens with other fixtures, too, such as faucets. Or electronic appliances. I usually did not notice it until Cas interrupted whatever I was doing, to point it out to me.

Partly due to exchanges like that, Cas regularly referred to me as a witch during our marriage. He often described me, quasi-affectionately, as "witching" people and things. It was certainly not the worst thing he ever called me: less than a year ago, at the time of this writing, he stood in the street and screamed, "You fucking cunt, *I hope you die,*" at me, while holding my terrified, crying daughter. No matter how carefully, quietly, or gently I learned to tell Cas things he didn't want to hear, there was no extinguishing the ever-simmering rage that seems innate to his person. In this instance, he was angry over being legally compelled to pay for expenses he was in fact responsible to pay. The amount of money was fairly negligible; but for Cas, withholding money means exerting power. When he finally lost that kind of power over me, legally, it made him the angriest I've ever seen him. "I'm glad I got rid of your stupid fucking garden, you filthy whore," he leered at me, during a separate conversation around the same time. During the last year of our marriage, he had thrown away about twenty pots of herbs and flowers that I had grown from seed. My mother had gifted me the seeds, soil, and pots. Cas had initially brought a little cart home for me to keep the plants in. But, as the garden began to blossom, Cas increasingly considered it a frivolous and inappropriate use of my time and energy.

Perhaps it's true: I am a witch. And I am finally beginning to step into my power, in part by honoring my connection to the earth—my abilities to create, nurture, and sustain life. I am better protecting myself and cleansing my spaces of destructive influence. But definitions of witch are nebulous, fraught: Manson instructed the women who carried out the Cielo Drive murders to "leave a sign" and to "make it something witchy." This is how they came to write PIG on the door in Sharon Tate's blood, after she and her infant died while she screamed for her mother, fading out under the brutality of these women and the man they followed—the man, some might argue, under whose spell they had fallen. *Full of broken thoughts/ I cannot repair.*

***

In 2008, I spent Labor Day Weekend with my friend Gaitree. We ran a few errands, went to random places. On three separate occasions in the same day, birds appeared directly in our path, dead and decapitated.

I do not want to phrase it that way—that they appeared. But I am not sure how else to say it. We were walking, and the path ahead was clear, and then suddenly we would nearly fall over ourselves and each other trying not to step on the dead bird that was suddenly underneath our feet.

We wondered if a cat had torn off the heads off of the birds. We told ourselves, and each other, that that had to be it. Neither of us had seen any cats.

Unnerved, we mentioned the odd sequence to Gaitree's parents, who explained that, on the Vedic calendar, we were about to enter a time of upheaval, tumult, and destruction. The earth was going to cleanse itself, they said, but a lot of suffering, war, disease, poverty, and other problems were the route to that cleansing. *A lot of people are going to die,* they said. Gaitree and I were terrified. Her mother said that the sign was perhaps shown to us so that we would not need to be so afraid—so that we would understand that what was about to happen would have a purpose.

***

After Cas's public threat, my divorce attorney advised me to file a police report for harassment. She forwarded me police reports from prior years against Cas, which she had obtained from several different local police departments. Several of the reports detailed Cas's history of violence. Women I didn't know contacted me unsolicited to share stories of violence, of injury at his hands. Unnerved by these revelations, I asked my friend Saumya, a religious scholar at Harvard University and ordained clergy, about possibilities for spiritual protection.

Case

Case Number: redacted
Location:

Reporting Officer ID:

Incident Type: Burglary - Residential
Occurred From:
Occurred Thru: redacted
Disposition: Arrest / Adult
Disposition Date:
Reported Date: redacted

Offenses

No.	Group/ORI	Crime Code	Statute	Description	Counts
1		redacted		BURG DWELLING CAUSING INJURY	1

Subjects

Type	No. Name	Address	Phone	Race	Sex	DOB/Age
Suspect				White	Male	
		redacted				
Victim				White	Male	
Victim				White	Female	

"I think even if they did arrest him for harassment, it probably wouldn't be enough for any sort of meaningful conviction," I said. "Like, I'm not sure it will actually solve anything, and I'm not sure it's worth the risk of making him even more erratic and volatile. I have a daughter to protect."

"I understand," she said. "And you have a self to protect, too. This must be terrifying for you. But Fox, listen to me: even if the police can't do anything right now, you do have a system in place to protect you. You have a justice system. Hear what I'm telling you. You're going to be kept safe."

A few months later—on the first day of March 2020—a red-breasted robin flew into the window next to my front door. His neck broken, he dropped dead onto the front porch. I was at home, but didn't recognize the sound for what it signified. I thought a local religious zealot, who throughout my life has occasionally attempted to convert me, might have stopped by, knocked, and given up when I didn't answer. I don't know why I thought that, or why the thought didn't seem strange or upsetting to me. I found the bird that way, a few hours later. At first, I thought I was going to have to kill it, to put it out of its misery. As I lifted him off of the floor, the angle of his neck indicated that he was no longer in his body.

I found a shoebox, and lined it with tissue paper and plastic bags. I put the shoebox into yet another plastic bag. I hoped it would keep him warm. I knew he was dead, but I believe it must take some time for the soul to fully pass from the body.

The next week, our national lockdowns began. A few days into quarantine, I spoke to Gaitree on the telephone.

"A dead bird showed up on my doorstep last week," she said.

"Mine, too," I said. "A robin. I buried him."

"I didn't think to bury mine," she said. "But I hope we can stop seeing dead birds soon."

"I hope so too," I said.

NARRATIVE FOR CASE #

Created 12/15
Last Changed 12/15

arresting officer's name redacted CONDUCTED A TRAFFIC STOP OF A VEHICLE WAS OPERATING FORFAILING TO STOP AT A STOP SIGN AT THE INTERSECTION OF ST AND ST. THE VEHICLE WAS STOPPED IN FRONT OF AVE. WAS TAKEN INTO CUSTODY FOR CRIMINAL POSSESSION OF A WEAPON, A BILLYCLUB WAS IN PLAIN VIEW BEHIND THE DRIVER'S SEAT. A BOTTLE OF JACK DANIELSWHISKEY WAS ALSO IN PLAIN VIEW BEHIND THE DRIVER'S SEAT. WAS ASKED IF THERE WAS ANYTHING ELSE IN THE VEHICLE THAT WAS ILLEGALTO POSSESS. STATED THAT THERE WAS A PIPE IN THE CENTERCONSOLE AND THAT THERE WAS POSSIBLY SOME CONDUCTED A SEARCH OF THE VEHICLE AND LOCATED THE PIPE AND A QUANTITY OF .

INPLAIN VIEW BEHIND THE DRIVER'S SEAT THE BOTTLE OF JACK DANIEL'S HAD BEENOPENED AND WAS ABOUT ONE QUARTER FULL. ADMITTED THAT THE JACKDANIEL'S WAS HIS.

TURNED OVER A PAIR OF BRASS METAL KNUCKLES THAT HE HAD IN HIS FRONTRIGHT PANTS POCKET. ARRESTED FOR CRIMINAL POSSESSION OFA WEAPON WAS ADVISED OF HIS MIRANDA RIGHTS AND A VOLUNTARY STATEMENT WAS OBTAINEDFROM . WAS PROCESSED AND LATER RELEASED ON BAIL.

CLOSED BY ARREST.

***

In late October of 2012, I was living in upstate New York with Cas, as he narrowly avoided multiple assault charges and casually introduced me to two uxoricides. During this time, the poet Elizabeth Cantwell and I were trying to write a hybrid visual-and-lyric poem about 10050 Cielo Drive and its existential significance to Los Angeles.

I made a painting for the work. I custom-mixed several different shades of red and of brown—probably about twenty, in total—and I finger-painted the word "PIG," among other things, on a plain white piece of canvas. I felt uncomfortable as I designed it in my mind, and physically cold as I mixed the colors. I felt sick as I began to paint. I was nauseous and shaking by the time I finished.

Because I felt so physically wrong, I knew I had to get rid of the painting. But I also knew I hadn't put myself through all of that for nothing. You suffer for your fucking art. I took a high-resolution photograph of my painting, to use for the hybrid piece.

My camera cooperated in taking the photograph. Then, immediately after I snapped the final photograph, it shut off. After three tries, it turned on and I could see that it had saved the images. I knew it must be a basic mechanical issue, but that didn't make me feel any better.

My computer shut down twice as I tried to transfer the photos. Both times it turned itself off. I didn't have it in me to try a third time. I had heard things about solar flares, and dimly wondered whether we were having one, or something like that. I felt a sharp pain on top of my head. I wondered if this was what it felt like to dissociate. The lights went out in the hallway. I forced myself up out of the chair, and left.

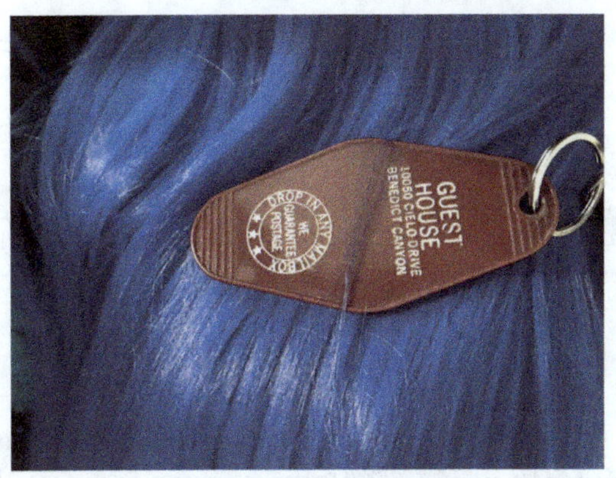

***

I have a private theory about Charlie Manson: I think when he and Charles Manson stumbled around the desert hallucinating together, the psychoactive drugs they'd taken and the purifying, sacred desert heat combined to bless Charlie Manson with a vision. I think he looked into Charles Manson's eyes and saw himself—a man who shared his name, his age, and the more general characteristics of his physical appearance. I think Charles Manson told Charlie Manson, wordlessly, about his plans for the future: the race war he wanted to start, the tyrannical power he intended to seize. I think Charlie first saw a recognizable kind of pleasure in Manson's eyes when their trip started, but then, as future events unfolded in tableau before Charlie, he saw that pleasure twist and mutate into narcissistic sadism, into something psychotic, something most of us can't fully understand and so we call it evil. I think that Charlie Manson was looking into a mirror forged in hell, and that he realized if he didn't get away now, Charles Manson was going to reach right through, grab him by the throat, and pull him through the looking-glass, past an event horizon he did not want to cross but knew he could. Perhaps, on the other side of this transparent portal, he saw the body of a woman like me, hurt in the ways that Cas hurt me, killed in the ways Cas threatened to kill me. Is the significant difference between a man like Cas and a man like Charlie simply that Charlie chose to run away from his violent potential, rather than towards it?

I was standing at the bar name redacted threw a can of beer at Me. The can of beer struck me in the Mouth causing a large gash to the right side of my lower lip and a smaller gash to the ~~top~~ right side of my upper lip. I want to press charges for the incident. this statement is true to the best of my Knowledge. I have been given the opportunity to change and review this statement.

to the right side of his upper lip. Medics responded on scene and told complainant he should go to the hospital as he needs stitches but he refused to go to the hospital. Photographs were taken on scene of victim's injuries and tagged into evidence.

And you could have it all/ my empire of dirt.

***

It's become de rigeuer in secular fashion for young women to brand themselves, especially on social media, as witchy. They don't always mean something as religiously or culturally specific as Wiccan or Bruja or Occultist. They sometimes mean, more broadly, that they are spiritually empowered and enlightened. They sometimes simply mean, with less articulation, that they are powerful. And, of course, the cultural trope of the sexy witch has been vacillating through mainstream popularity for decades now. I think this is perhaps, in part, because women in our culture are so often reduced to their sexuality in a way that's intended to degrade and control—*a fucking bitch* (literally, a dog in heat) or a *fucking cunt* (literally, just a body part to be used for a single purpose, by a man, and then discarded, by a man), both of which Cas called me in front of our daughter on more than one occasion. We are so often told, in daily circumstances and quotidian language that our bodies are not our own, and that a man can sneeringly wrest agency from us to prove it—that we sometimes forget, as a cohort, that taking control of our own bodies and sexualities is only one small aspect of stepping into our full power. Bodied autonomy is only the first moment of the transformation we have begun to come together to enact.

Seeing me as a "witch"—a woman whose energy could literally or figuratively light up (or darken) a room, call familiars, bring her dreams of things yet to unfold in gorgeous, Technicolor detail—didn't stop Cas from grabbing me by my hair and licking my face to degrade me, when he was angry and drunk and wanted to punish me for "disrespecting" him by leaving the crock pot dirty in the sink overnight. It didn't stop him from threatening to smash my laptop, or from throwing food all over the walls in a fit of rage and and forcing me to clean it as punishment. For him, my spirituality was a bangle, a parlor trick, a kitschy figurine purchased on the boardwalk.

I needed to learn how to access and wield that spiritual power myself, so that I could see and understand myself as powerful. Cas wanted to prevent that: he didn't want me to have any recourse against the physical intimidation he presented, or his institutionalized privilege. When he sneered at me, tauntingly, "You're a *cunt*," he meant that he had the ability to obliterate my identity and replace it with whatever he cared to write in the blank space he'd created. During our marriage, he told me several times that because he "only" called me cunt "a few times a year," that I needed to learn to live with it. He told me that calmly, in a tone that could have been mistaken for conciliatory by someone who didn't understand the actual diction leaving his mouth. I'd seen him as a protector, at the beginning of our relationship; I didn't realize until it was too late that the price he intended to exact in exchange was ownership of me, and my body.

PRELIMINARY BREATH TESTING (PBT):

Name redacted **was requested to provide a sample of his breath for the preliminary test of blood alcohol content utilizing a device approved for this purpose.** Redacted **agreed to provide this sample which showed his BAC to be .193%.**

's Physical Presentation:

- **He was unbalanced.**
- **I smelt an odor of alcoholic beverage coming from his mouth when he spoke.**
- **His eyes were bloodshot and glossy and watery.**
- **potentially identifying physical detail reacted**
- **His eyelids were droopy**
- **Speech slurred**

***

For women, for non-binary people, for people of color, for queer people—those of us with marginalized bodies, whose entire complex human identities are often oppressively reduced to one or a few aspects of our physical bodies—because to reduce us to those and to institutionalize those definitions is a form of total domination of our bodies, our selves—our systems of faith are our justice systems. Our ancestors, spiritually purified through the rituals of death, stand behind us and help us. Because they, too, have lived with their bodies through the experience of our institutionalized justice systems failing us so frequently. And, as Audre Lorde writes, though our silence will not protect us, "for every real word spoken, for every attempt I had ever made to speak those truths for which I am still seeking, I had made contact with other women while we examined the words to fit a world in which we all believed, bridging our differences."

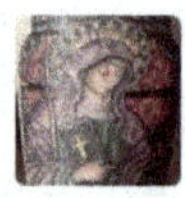

Hide details

To:

Date: June 8 9:44 AM

In case I ever need it archived, this is what did to the bedroom door because we had a minor argument (he thought I was being too quiet and something might be wrong; when I said no, there was actually nothing wrong, he accused me of lying and then of being mean to him and wouldn't let it go) and I tried to leave and go into the bedroom to get away from the conversation. It terrified me and he seemed fine with that. I decided I better make a record now in case he gets worse. I'm still terrified.

Sent from my iPhone

Because of traumatic bonding, and because I grew to fear the man I loved, it took me a long time to learn that I did not need to persuade Cas of my power; I needed to persuade myself. And I could not do that by remaining silent, even when I realized in terror that the center had not held—had, rather than holding fast, shattered into celestial artifacts that whirl lonely through the cosmos, tearing through the sky as they seek & seek & seek until they burn themselves up, or collide with something larger and create further oblivion. And when I realized that I was too exhausted to keep trying to hold on to any of those furiously tearing fragments of what the center of my universe once was. That the center was not coming back. That what I believed to be the center would never exist again—had possibly never existed, except in my mind.

***

I still dream, sometimes, about the little girl who was taken away from the Bird House. She was obviously unstable, but what happened to make her that way? Why did she think her adoptive parents wanted to kill her? Did she really need to drink the blood of a sacrificial animal "for strength"? Against what? If she could call birds, could she also talk to cats? In many religious traditions that incorporate animal sacrifice, it is believed that specific animals, for spiritual reasons of their own and out of cosmic love for human beings, volunteer for the job.

Why, in the end, do witches call spirit familiars? We think of cats and birds and predator and prey, as mortal enemies—not unlike the way we have accepted the idea of two different "species" of women and pitted them against each other. Blonde and brunette. Madonna and whore. Cats and birds are often presented in a similar dichotomy, though both are associated with the feminine. Cats are presented as an archetypal aggressor—ruthless, stealthy, beautiful, slinking, intelligent, vicious—while birds are stereotypical victims—gentle, beautiful, stupid, fragile, vulnerable. But consider, for example, the cassowary. Consider the sackful of kittens sunk in a lake. Perhaps witches call both cats and birds because we understand all too well what men have done to them. And perhaps they understand this too, which is why the familiars we call will protect us. And the way in which they protect us is very special, though not entirely dissimilar from the covenant that humans have shared with many species of animal for thousands of years: they are willing to sacrifice themselves for us. If we need them to, they would spill their own blood in order to defend us. They spring from the same earth that nurtures us as we nurture it. That provides sustenance and gives us limits when we are transgressing too destructively as a cohort. By tooth and claw and spilled blood, they do their best to keep us safe in a world that is hostile to our bodies. And so, you see: my belief system is not singularly my protection, or my community, or my faith, or my understanding of sacrifice: it is also my justice system. And, because it bears a name that identifies my power, both to me and to others, it is also a source of my power. Come with your torches. I'm not afraid. I live in the Shadow Hills, where it's always fire season.

Author's note: Some of the names in this essay have been changed to protect the privacy of the guilty. Additionally, some of the names in this essay have been changed to protect the privacy of their victims.

Notes

"Won't you bury me/ beneath the tree/ where my family lies/ hear the willow cry" is a phrase from the Steeldrivers' song, "Hear the Willow Cry."

"Singer-sewing contest, soap box derby, eating or drinking (pie watermelon), diaper derby palisades, walkathon St Louis, chess champ, miss appetite, miss fluidless contact lens, yeast raised donut queen, miss peel appeal natl idaho potato week, tooth health week queen, miss press photog, miss antifreeze, miss saltwater taffy wk" is a list found in one of Diane Arbus' notebooks, reminding herself of potential future subjects for photography projects.

"Will the circle be unbroken/ by and by, Lord, by and by?/ There's a better home a-waiting/ in the sky, Lord, in the sky" are lines from "Will the Circle Be Unbroken," a Christian hymn written in 1907, later adapted into the bluegrass music tradition for secular performance.

"One by one, we'll gain the portals/ there to dwell with the immortals" and "that land beyond the river" are lines from the Christian hymn "When They Ring The Golden Bells," written in 1887, later adapted into the bluegrass tradition for secular performance.

"Everywhere in the world, they hurt little girls," is a line spoken by Cersei Lannister on *Game of Thrones*, in "First of His Name," S4E5.

"Peter Was One of Four Catholic Workers in Upstate New York Who Spilled His Blood at a Military Recruitment Center to Protest the USA's Invasion of Iraq, and Was Subsequently Arrested and Imprisoned," contains my own paraphrase of the following verses from the *New Oxford Annotated Bible*:

> 2 Peter 2:17: "These are waterless springs and mists driven by a storm; for them the deepest darkness has been reserved."
> 2 Peter 2:22: "It has happened to them according to the true proverb, 'The dog turns back to its own vomit,' and 'the sow is washed only to wallow in the mud.'"

> 2 Peter 3:5-7: "They deliberately ignore this fact, that by the word of God heavens existed long ago and an earth was formed out of water and by means of water, through which the world of that time was deluged with water and perished. But by the same word the present heavens and earth have been reserved for fire, being kept until the day of judgment and destruction of the godless."

"Aubrenwing" is a neologism, naming the space between sea and sky that you can find yourself flying into if you look too long at the horizon.

"Everywhere in the World, They Hurt Little Girls" contains deliberate echoes of WCW and Elizabeth Bishop, intended to draw out bitter contextual ironies.

"The Raven-Haired Seer Visits the Abandoned NXIVM Headquarters" contains fractured retellings of several New Testament parables: Parable of the Strong Man, Parable of the Leaven, Parable of the Mustard Seed, and Parable of the Glass Jar.

"For here there is no place that does not see you. You must change your life." is from Stephen Mitchell's translation of Rainer Maria Rilke's poem, "Archaic Torso of Apollo," alluded to via paraphrase in the poem, "The Raven-Haired Seer Draws a Card from Her Own Handmade Oracle Deck."

"Women don't fear pain the way men do; they have to be broken in other ways," is a line from *Orange Is the New Black*, S5E10, "The Reverse Midas Touch," which is alluded to via paraphrase in "The Sunny-Haired Undertaker's Daughter and the Raven-Haired Cartographers' Daughter Write Letters Amidst the Pandemic."

"I've been up all night, talking, talking, reading the Kaddish aloud," is a line from Allen Ginsberg's poem "Kaddish," paraphrased in the final "Exodus in X Minor" poem.

"Somewhere, someone is traveling furiously towards you, at incredible speed," is a line from John Ashbery's poem, "At North Farm," paraphrased in the final "Exodus in X Minor" poem.

Acknowledgments

The author gratefully acknowledges all of the organizations, institutions, journals, magazines, and individuals who have supported this work through publication, time, space, energy, or other resources.

Several of the poems in this collection first appeared in the following journals, sometimes in slightly different forms: *Luna Luna, Menacing Hedge, PITH, RE:AL,* and *Yes Poetry*. Several of them also appeared in *Exodus in X Minor,* winner of the 2014 Sundress Publications Chapbook Prize.

Thank you to Beth Couture for selecting *Exodus in X Minor* as a chapbook contest winner. You changed my life.

Thank you to the University of Southern California for the fellowships, particularly the Provost's Fellowship and Travel Research Grants that made it possible for me to focus on writing the first drafts of the poems that comprised my chapbook *Exodus in X Minor,* many of which subsequently also appear in this book, many in somewhat altered forms. Thank you to the English and Creative Writing Program in particular for the additional Departmental Fellowships that helped make this work possible.

Thank you to both David St. John and Mark Irwin for their feedback and guidance on the early versions of those same poems that comprised *Exodus in X Minor* and are now included in this book. Thank you both also for making sure I didn't get derailed from my career early on due to trauma.

Thank you to Sarah Reck for her gorgeous design work.

Thanks to Sarah Clark for her keen editorial eye, which was indispensable in helping me distill "I Live in the Shadow Hills" into something other people could read and make sense of.

My sincere thanks to Jen Fitzgerald, Jessica Walsh, and Letitia Trent, each of whom read and offered substantial feedback on "I Live in the Shadow Hills" at different points during the decade it took me to write it. Thanks also to Elizabeth Cantwell, who got my brain firing with a lot of these thoughts, questions, and impulses during our long-since-abandoned collaborative project *In This Chicken Coop*. There are surely appreciable threads of your influence in this essay, for which I'm quite grateful. Finally, my deepest thanks to Joanna C. Valente for reading the final version of the essay approximately eleventy-billion times, and to both Joanna and Lisa Marie Basile for giving it a home at *Luna Luna Magazine*.

My heartfelt thanks to Allison Joseph, Bhanu Kapil, Mary McMyne, Lynn Melnick, and Saba Razvi for the time they took to read this book and offer such kind words about it.

Thanks to Chard DeNiord and Bertha Rogers for their continuous literary friendship and support of my work over the years.

My deep and abiding gratitude both to and for Jasmine An and Mary McMyne, who helped shepherd the electric chaos of these poems into their final collective form.

Thank you to Randi DiMichiei and Yassin LaRoussi of Blood Honey for the absolutely stunning concept album they've created in *Fractured Temple*. I can't get over how beautiful these songs are, and I feel so honored that you wrote them as the soundtrack to *Raven King*.

Joanna C. Valente, you have my deep gratitude as a Yes Poetry author, my respect and admiration as a creative collaborator, and my huge friendship love as a regular human wandering around this strange world. Thank you for being a talented, insightful editor, a brilliant poet and artist, and a wonderful, thoughtful, funny, kind, loyal friend. Thank you for giving me the artistic safe space and support in which *Raven King* came to exist. This book would very literally never have existed without you. There are no words that could properly quantify the joy our writerly friendship (and, following from that, regular human friendship) has brought me. Thank you, too, for the gorgeous illustrations in *Raven King* that help make it the best book it could possibly be.

Sky-big love and gratitude for my almost improbably beautiful village of family, friends, and loved ones—without whom I would definitely not still be on this plane of existence. I love you all so very much. If your name belongs in these pages and you don't see it, please know that it's due to my own tired memory synapses, never a lack of love.

Karli Myers and Julia Adams, thank you for making upstate New York a more hospitable place than I might otherwise have first found it when I moved here. Saumya Arya Haas, Sallie Ann Glassman, Shannon Lee: thank you for your protection and love, you stunning visionaries. Shannon Hardwick, Jenny MacBain-Stephens, Jasmine An, Mary McMyne, Katie Manning, Cee Martinez, Randi DiMichiei, Nadia Gerassimenko, Michael Simon: members of my witchy art family, sometimes from afar or with long pauses in the conversations. Love you bunches.

Sammie Jamieson, thanks for saving my life with your friendship and your love and your truly amazing second sight. I adore you.

Sarah Lewin, Megan Peil, Gaitree Singh, Carlene Miller, Mike Coury, Jessie Coleman: friends for the ages. Thank you for the shapes & spaces you take up in my life. I love you.

Norah Henry, Sheila Henry, Bobbie Johnson, Linda Phillips, Caiolinn Ertel: thank you all for your strength, clarity, kindness, love, and support.

My daughter, for being her beautiful, luminous self and the most amazing little soul to share life with. My parents and siblings, for their love and support. My grandparents and great-grandparents and great-greats, going back, for their legacies. My dogs and my gardens, for keeping me anchored. My ghosts, for keeping me unmoored.

Finally, inevitably, I hold in my heart the deepest devotion for my ancestors, my lwa, my saints, my spirits, and Spirit. I would be nothing without You. May the circle be unbroken, by and by.

Biographical Notes

About the Author

Fox Henry Frazier is a poet and essayist whose first book, *The Hydromantic Histories*, was selected by Vermont Poet Laureate Chard deNiord as recipient of the 2014 Bright Hill Poetry Award. Her second poetry collection, *Like Ash in the Air After Something Has Burned* (2017), was nominated for an Elgin Award. She edited the anthologies *Among Margins: Critical and Lyrical Writing on Aesthetics* and *Political Punch: Contemporary Poems on the Politics of Identity.*

Fox was graduated Phi Beta Kappa from Binghamton University, and was honored with fellowships at Columbia University, where she received her MFA. She was Provost's Fellow at the University of Southern California, where she earned a PhD in Literature and Creative Writing and served as Poetry Editor of Gold Line Press and a Founding & Managing Editor of Ricochet Editions.

Fox created the small literary press Agape Editions, which she currently manages with the poet and scholar Jasmine An. She lives in upstate New York with her daughter, her dogs, her gardens, and her ghosts.

About the Illustrator

Joanna C. Valente is a human who lives in Brooklyn, New York. Joanna is the author of *Sirs & Madams, The Gods Are Dead, Marys of the Sea, Xenos, Sexting Ghosts, No(body)*, and *A Love Story* (Vegetarian Alcoholic Press, 2021). They are the editor of *A Shadow Map: Writing By Survivors of Sexual Assault* and the illustrator of *Dead Tongue*, a poetry collection by Bunkong Tuon (Yes Poetry, 2020). Joanna received a MFA in writing at Sarah Lawrence College and a double BA in creative writing and literature at SUNY Purchase College. Currently, Joanna is the founder of Yes Poetry and the senior managing editor for *Luna Luna Magazine.*

Biographical Note

Artists' Statement on the Soundtrack

Randi DeMichiei and Yassin Laroussi are independent artists and healers who live in upstate New York and record under the name Blood Honey. A chance meeting was the catalyst that led these like-minded, lifelong musicians to collaborate on a soundtrack for the release of *Raven King* by Fox Henry Frazier, with compositions derived from her work. Titled *Fractured Temple,* Blood Honey's debut album represents the duo's eclectic sound and efforts to bring the listener under the wing of the Raven King.

Colophon

This book was set in the typefaces Amiri, IM Fell English SC, and Passion One.

Amiri, the body text of this book, was designed by software developer Dr. Khaled Hosny. Amiri is a revival of a classical Arabic typeface in Naskh style, originally pioneered in the early 20th century by Bulaq Press in Cairo. Bulaq Press was also known as Amiria Press, after which the font is named. Amiri balances the beauty of Naskh calligraphy with the constraints of elegant typography. The original version was one of the few metal typefaces used in setting the Qur'an, and Amiri was created as a digital typeface that could be used for this purpose as well. Amiri is a publicly available font, and was itself developed and published exclusively with free software. Its designer, Dr. Hosny, is based in Egypt, where he works as a type designer and font engineer for the virtual type foundry AlifType.

IM Fell English SC, which was used for titles and headings in this book and the author's name on the front cover, was created by Italian designer and civil engineer Igino Marini. Marini heavily researched the original Fell types that were painstakingly constructed and became popular in 1600s England. These were created by John Fell, and bequeathed by him to Oxford University upon his death in 1686. After completing the necessary research, Marini digitized the fonts in the year 2000. IM Fell English SC conveys love of beauty, particularly the beauty found in tradition and erudition. Marini was born in Italy in 1964, and in addition to his primary career as a civil engineer, he has created several other fonts and digital works, including iKern, the autospacing and autokerning tool he designed in 2002.

Passion One, used for the book's title on the front cover, was designed in 2011, by Alejandro Lo Celso. Alejandro Lo Celso developed this font as part of his work through FontStage, a group of independent Latin American type designers who create original fonts for the web and print industry. Passion One was developed for the specific purpose of composing titles in big sizes. As its name makes clear, it was intended to convey passion for one's ideas—the minute counterforms remove as much negative space as possible, giving a sense of concrete, tangible results and the forward momentum that can only be achieved through the fervor of inspired dedication. Alejandro Lo Celso is an Argentinean designer. In 2001, he founded PampaType, the first Argentinean type foundry, where he remains principal today.

The typography and binding design of this book were created by Sarah Reck in Pittsburgh, Pennsylvania, in autumn of 2021. Her design work can be viewed most prominently for Hyacinth Girl Press.

YESPOETRY

Yes Poetry is an art lifestyle magazine and literary publisher for people who don't fit in, who want to challenge themselves, who are interested in activism, occultism, art, feminism, queer community, camp + glam, and crave intellectual and creative stimulation.

We are for the outcasts—for the kind of people who don't settle, the kind of people who dream, people who want to make the world a better place for everyone.
The answer is yes.

www.ingramcontent.com/pod-product-compliance
Lightning Source LLC
LaVergne TN
LVHW020509100826
845148LV00003B/737
* 9 7 8 0 5 7 8 9 9 5 4 0 3 *